The Marvels of Divine Grace

The Marvels of Divine Grace

REVISED, ADAPTED AND MODERNIZED
BY
MONSIGNOR WM. J DOHENY, C.S.C.

ASSOCIATE JUSTICE EMERITUS OF THE TRIBUNAL
OF THE SACRED ROMAN ROTA

FIRST PRESIDENT OF THE CANON LAW
SOCIETY OF AMERICA

FORMER PROFESSOR OF LEGAL DEONTOLOGY
OF THE SCHOOL OF LAW OF THE
UNIVERSITY OF NOTRE DAME

FORMER ASSISTANT GENERAL OF THE
CONGREGATION OF HOLY CROSS

IMPRIMATUR OF 1917 EDITION

Nihil Obstat:
   HENRY G. S. BOWDEN,
      Censor Deputatus

Imprimatur:
   EDM. CAN. SURMONT,
      Vicarius Generalis

Westmonasterii,
   Die 16 Augustii, 1917

Revised Edition,
   Pro Manuscripto
Feast of the Assumption
   of Our Lady,
      August 15, 1977

Printed by Ave Maria Press, Notre Dame, Indiana 46556

Table of Contents

CHAPTER III

ON THE EFFECTS AND FRUITS OF DIVINE GRACE

CHAPTER IV

ON SOME PREROGATIVES OF DIVINE GRACE

CHAPTER V

OUR LADY INTRODUCES US TO THE LIFE OF DIVINE GRACE

CHAPTER VI

OUR LADY LEADS US TO PERFECTION

Preface

Exactly sixty years ago, an English edition of *Del Aprecio y Estima de la Divina Gracia* first published in Madrid in 1638 by Father John Eusebius Nieremberg, S.J., was printed in England and published in New York under the title: *The Marvels of Divine Grace.*

Father John E. Nieremberg was an ascetical writer who was born in Madrid, Spain, in 1595 of a Tyrolese father and Bavarian mother and spent his life in Spain and died in Madrid on April 7, 1658. He was a renowned spiritual director and the author of many works dealing with the ascetical and mystical doctrine of the Church. He also wrote a life of St. Ignatius and several volumes of biographies of saints and saintly men of the Jesuit Order. Despite the fact that he was a prolific author, he is unfortunately little known in the English-speaking world, so much so that he is not even mentioned in the *New Catholic Encyclopedia.*

It appears that the *Marvels of Divine Grace* was never reprinted in English after the 1917 edition. Like many other spiritual classics this volume simply disappeared from libraries and bookshelves. Unfortunately, many Christians and even priests and religious seem to forget the real meaning and import of divine grace. We too often forget that divine grace elevates us from the moment of our baptism above the natural order to a heavenly plane that is sublimely and infinitely higher. It uplifts us high above nature and can come only from God, thereby enabling us to perform actions deserving of a heavenly reward. It makes us children of God, living temples of the Holy Spirit and "sharers of the divine nature" as St. Peter reminds us (II Peter 1:4). Furthermore, it endows us with the keenest spiritual insight and makes us in a most special way beloved friends of God, upon whom he looks with particular interest and over whom he watches with loving and fatherly solicitude.

Many modern writers give us reams of cheerless chaff cleverly written but almost totally devoid of vital doctrine. The purpose of this small volume is to stir the heart and uplift the soul in gratitude to God for the truly wonderful and crowning gift of his ineffable goodness to humankind. It aims to place readers in the intimate presence of Jesus himself so that they can say like the disciples of Emmaus: "Were not our hearts burning inside us as he talked to us on the road and explained the Scriptures to us?" (Luke 24:32).

In an effort to revive interest in deeply spiritual works, this recognized classic is being printed at my own expense for private circulation in the hope that it will help many souls who are really seeking a closer union with God. If only one immortal soul is saved or sanctified by this volume, our efforts will be more than compensated.

Monsignor Wm. J. Doheny, C.S.C.
Palazzo San Callisto
Piazza San Callisto, 16
00120 — CITTA' DEL VATICANO, S.C.V., Europe

FEAST OF THE ASSUMPTION OF OUR LADY
AUGUST 15, 1977

"What father among you will give his son a snake if he asks for a fish, or hand him a scorpion if he asks for an egg? If you, with all your sins, know how to give your children good things, how much more will the heavenly Father give the Holy Spirit to those who ask him" (Luke 11:11-13).

"In contrast, the fruit of the spirit is love, joy, peace, patient endurance, kindness, generosity, faith, mildness, and chastity" (Gal. 5:22-23).

I

On the Nature of Divine Grace

1. THE HEAVENLY VALUE OF DIVINE GRACE

2. THE INEFFABLE MARVELS OF DIVINE GRACE

3. THE SUBLIME MYSTERY OF THE INFUSION AND COMMUNICATION OF DIVINE GRACE

4. GRACE IS GLORY IN EXILE, GLORY IS DIVINE GRACE AT HOME

5. PARTICIPATION BY GRACE IN THE DIVINE NATURE

6. DIVINE GRACE IS THE PLEDGE OF FUTURE GLORY

7. INFINITE DISTANCE BETWEEN GOD AND HUMAN BEINGS

8. SANCTIFYING GRACE AS A SHARING IN THE TRANSCENDING HOLINESS OF GOD

9. TRANSFORMATION IN CHRIST BY DIVINE GRACE

10. EVERY SUPERNATURAL ACTION MERITS AN INCREASE OF DIVINE GRACE

11. THE SUBLIME INTERCHANGE OF HEAVENLY GIFTS IN THE INCARNATION

12. THE MYSTERIES OF THE INCARNATION AND THE DIVINE MOTHERHOOD OF MARY

13. DIVINE GRACE IS THE PEARL OF GREAT PRICE

On the Nature of Divine Grace

1. THE HEAVENLY VALUE OF DIVINE GRACE

The grace of God is a ray of divine beauty infused from heaven into the immortal soul of man, and penetrating its innermost nature with such brilliancy and power that the soul delights the eye of God, is most tenderly loved by him, is adopted as his child, and is elevated above natural limits from earth to heaven. By grace the soul is received into the bosom of the Eternal Father, and at the side of his Son, participates in his nature, his life and glory, and inherits the realms of his eternal happiness.

St. Thomas Aquinas, the Angel of the Schools (Thom., I, 9, 113, a. 9, ad 2), teaches that the whole world and all it contains is of less value before God than the divine grace of one human being. St. Augustine maintains that the whole of heaven, together with all Angels, cannot compare with it (Aug., I ad Bonif., c. 6). How infinitely superior in value, therefore, is divine grace to all the riches and pleasures of the world! And yet how often do human beings, more rash and foolish than Esau, lose an inheritance immeasurably greater than his for the sake of a momentary enjoyment!

"Be amazed at this, O heavens, and shudder with sheer horror," says the Lord (Jeremiah 2:12). We disregard divine grace because we permit ourselves to be too deeply impressed by our senses with the transitory things of this life, and have but a superficial knowledge of true heavenly things. If we did but approach the inexhaustible fountain of divine grace, we should learn to esteem and admire it, and accordingly, as St. John Chrysostom says, we should carefully and zealously guard it. Let us, then, with the divine assistance, begin "to praise the glorious favor he has bestowed on us" (Eph. 1:6).

2. THE INEFFABLE MARVELS OF DIVINE GRACE

The least prerogative of divine grace is that it is infinitely above all natural things. " 'Heaven and earth shall pass away,' according to the assurance of our Savior," says St. Augustine, "but the salvation and justice of the elect will remain; for the former contain only the works of God, the latter the image of God" (Aug., tr. 72 in Joannem). St. Thomas, again, teaches that it is a greater work to bring a sinner back to grace than to create heaven and earth. For the objects of the latter work are temporary; the former work is so much greater because it leads to the participation in the immutable divine nature. In creation God erects for himself a dwelling only. In giving man a rational nature he places his servants and his creatures in this dwelling, but when he gives man his precious grace he receives him into his bosom, makes him his child, and communicates to him his own eternal life.

Again, divine grace is a gift which no created nature can possess of itself, or even lay claim to, for it belongs alone, properly speaking, to the highest nature of God himself. Thus, theologians maintain that God cannot produce a created being that would from its nature already possess divine grace. The Church accordingly teaches that neither man nor any other creature bears in his nature even the least germ of divine grace. St. Augustine remarks that nature is related to grace in the same way as inanimate matter is to living organisms. Lifeless matter cannot itself give life, but must receive it from another living being. In like manner the rational creature has not of itself any special grace, and cannot acquire it by its own labor and merit. God alone can, from pure love, give this grace by opening the abyss of his omnipotence, and pouring out his divine power upon his creature. Grace is as a heavenly light which diffuses itself from the depths of the Divinity on the rational creature. The sun pours down its light on the earth, and our nature, like the earth, receives the rays of the Divine Sun and becomes glorified and illuminated by them. Now, as God, whom we possess by grace, not only contains within himself the perfection of all things, but is infinitely more perfect than all things put together, so divine grace is more precious than all created things. To despise these great gifts which are offered to us by God with such tender love would be to draw down upon ourselves the punishment of the men in the

Gospel, who, having been invited to the king's banquet, made frivolous excuses to stay away, and brought down his just ire upon them. Even if we do not go to the length of forfeiting all God's favor and his graces by mortal sin, still, what folly it would be if we abstained from the opportunities he gives us of increasing their precious store! Even if we do not offend God by omiting to assist at Mass on weekdays, or by neglecting an opportunity of prayer, or a work of mercy, or of self-abnegation or mortification, nevertheless, we suffer an immense loss if we do not increase this heavenly capital by these means, because the least degree of divine grace is worth more than all the riches of the world. We are not required to shed our blood in this labor. One sign is sufficient, one earnest resolution, one pious wish, the holy Name by which we express our love for him or invoke his assistance. Who would not gladly invoke Jesus a thousand times a day if he could thereby obtain as many coffers of gold? And yet what is gold untold in comparison to the spiritual treasures which God is prepared to bestow on us by means as simple and easy as these?

3. THE SUBLIME MYSTERY OF THE INFUSION AND COMMUNICATION OF DIVINE GRACE

St. Augustine, commenting upon our Lord's promises to his disciples, that they should do yet greater things than he had done, says this might be explained by the fact that St. Peter had healed the sick by his shadow passing over them, which we do not read of as happening to our Savior. "But it is more probable," he continues, "that we are to understand here the work of justification, in which we can co-operate for ourselves and others. For although we do not produce grace in ourselves, yet we can, with the divine assistance, prepare ourselves for it and make ourselves worthy of it. Likewise we may encourage and induce others to do the same, and thus we shall perform greater works than Christ did through his miracles" (Tr. 72 in Joannem). His miracles were for the most part worked on the body and on visible things, but by grace he works on the soul, he elevates it above its nature, implants in it the germ of a supernatural life, and reproduces, so to speak, himself in it by impressing upon it the image of his own divine nature. Accordingly the work of divine grace is the greatest wonder of God's omnipotence. It is greater than the creation of the world out of nothing, and can only be compared with the unspeakable act of God the Father in which he produced from all eternity his coequal Son, and in time united with him a human nature. As supernatural and sublime as is the generation of Christ, so is the infusion of divine grace into our souls, whereby, as St. Leo says, we participate in the generation of Christ.

In working miracles the Saints do but cooperate with God, who acts through and by means of them. But in grace we do more, because God wills that we should with his assistance prepare our souls for it, receive it from his hand, preserve, cultivate, and increase it.

How wonderful is this favor which God grants us of taking one soul to himself as his spouse, that by the power received from him she may produce in herself the image of God and become his child! Equally wonderful is the power which God has granted to his Church to communicate his divine grace to her children by her teaching and her sacraments. No greater work can be given to man to accomplish than to labor to acquire and increase grace in himself and in his fellowmen.

Oh if men could only realize the greatness of the act that is performed when by sincere contrition for their past sins they abandon their past and begin a new life: "If God has made you man," St. Augustine says, "and you, with God's help, make yourself a just man, your work is better than that of God" (Serm. 15, de verbis Apos.).

When our souls are in a state of grace, every degree of divine grace that we acquire raises us higher above our nature and unites us more closely to God. If we could reflect how every good work we perform has the power of increasing our grace, and thus adding to our eternal happiness, we should let no moments pass without loving God, adoring him, and uniting our acts and intentions with his. We should even rejoice with the Apostles that we are accounted worthy to suffer for the Name of Jesus.

The infusion and communication of grace is a miracle of the highest order: why does it not excite our wonder and admiration? Only because it is invisible to our corporal sight, and does not occur, like other miracles, rarely and exceptionally, but universally and according to fixed laws.

4. GRACE IS GLORY IN EXILE, GLORY IS DIVINE GRACE AT HOME

The glory of heaven, in which the blessed see and enjoy God, is nothing else but the fruition of the divine grace given to us here below. In other words, it can be said that: "Grace is glory in exile, glory is divine grace at home."

Divine grace is the fountain springing up unto everlasting life. It is the root of which the blossom and fruit is beatitude. "The wages of sin is death, but the grace of God life everlasting," says the Apostle. The Saints have continually been transported out of themselves at the contemplation of the reward which awaited them. St. Isidore wept over the necessity to eat, because he was compelled like animals to take bodily food, while he was destined for the banquet of the Blessed in heaven. But great as is the privilege of participating with the Saints in glory hereafter, there is yet a greater one. For by divine grace man participates in the uncreated divine nature. To speak in more precise terms: man in the state of grace is so superior to all created things because he is so near to God. He partakes of the prerogatives of God as a body partakes of the light and heat of fire in proportion to its proximity to the fire. The Fathers and Doctors of the Church are unanimous in ascribing this meaning to the words of St. Peter that, "by the most great and precious promises God has made us by Jesus Christ, we may be made partakers of the divine nature." From this we are to understand that the prerogatives which are above all created nature, and are due to the divine nature, are, as far as possible, communicated to our nature.

The Saints cannot find words to express the magnificence of this gift. St. Denis says: "Sanctity, or sanctifying grace, is a divine gift, an inexpressible copy of the highest Divinity and highest goodness, by means of which we enter a divine rank through a heavenly generation" (Eccl. hier., c. 2). Many of the holy Fathers teach with St. Thomas that by divine grace we are in a manner deified, and they apply to this mystery the words of our Savior: "I have said you are gods, and all of you sons of the most High" (Centur. oecon., I. 76).

"By the union with the Son and the Holy Spirit," says St. Cyril of Alexandria, "we all, who have believed and have been likened unto God, are partakers of the divine nature, not only in name, but in reality, because we have been glorified with a beauty surpassing all created beauty. For Christ is informed in us in an indescribable manner, not as one creature in another, but as God in created nature Christ transforms us, the creature, by the Holy Spirit into his image and elevates us to an uncreated dignity" (De Trin., i. 4).

"What is essential and substantial in God," says St. Thomas, "exists in the soul, which partakes by grace in the divine love, as a quality superadded to its nature" (I, 2, q. 110, art. 2, ad 2). Elsewhere the Angelical Doctor, in agreement with St. Basil, compares the soul to iron, which is in itself cold, black and hard, and without beauty, but when laid in a furnace becomes penetrated by its heat, and, without losing its own nature appears brilliant in color, flexible, and red-hot. God, we know, dwells in inaccessible light. He is to use our human words, a furnace of divine love. God thus, in descending to the creature he has made, or receiving him into his bosom, can without destroying the nature of man penetrate it with his divine light and warmth, so that its natural lowliness and defects disappear, and it is seemingly absorbed altogether in God.

5. PARTICIPATION BY GRACE IN THE DIVINE NATURE

Theologians say that a certain participation in the divine perfections is found in all things that God has created. All things more or less resemble God—in their existence, in their life, in their force, or activity. Therefore, as the Apostles teach, the invisible glory of God may be seen and considered in created things. But they differ much in their similarity. In material things we see but the print of his footsteps. They may reveal themselves as the work of his hands, but they do not represent his nature. Our souls and all pure spirits, such as the Angels, are by their very nature made to the likeness of the Divine Nature; for like God they are spiritual, rational, and possessed of free will. Yet their nature is finite, they are created out of nothing, and if not upheld by their Creator would fall back into nothingness.

The participation in the Divine Nature, therefore, which we enjoy by means of grace consists in this, that our nature assumes a condition peculiar to the Divine Nature, and becomes so similar to the Deity that, according to the Fathers of the Church, it is in a sense deified. We do not speak, therefore, of a dissolution of our substance in the divine substance or of a personal union with it, such as existed in our Divine Savior, but only of a glorification of our substance into the image of the Divine Nature. The truth lies in this—that we are made by the power and grace of God something which God alone is by nature. We are made to his likeness in a supernatural manner, and our soul receives a reflex of that glory which belongs to God alone.

To understand better this likeness to God, let us

examine the prerogatives which distinguish the divinity from created natures.

Let us first consider the eternal existence of God.

God exists by himself—eternal, immutable, and dependent on no one. Creatures are of themselves nothing. They only exist because God has created them and maintains them in existence. "I am who am," says the Lord. And "all nations are before him as if they had no being at all, and counted to him as nothing and vanity" (Isaiah 11:17). All creatures, even the immortal spirits, would in virtue of their nature fall back into nothingness if not sustained by the will of God and his good pleasure.

Grace therefore, according to St. Paul, is a new creation, and the foundation of a new indestructible kingdom, by means of which we are received into the bosom of the Eternal God by the side of the Eternal Word, by whose power the Father has created all things and who is coeternal with him (Eph. 2:10; Heb. 12:28). Thus, we are called to dwell in the tabernacle of God's eternity, at the fountain of all being and of all life. Here our eternal existence is as secure as that of God himself and we need fear neither death nor destruction. Were heaven and earth to pass away, the stars to fall from the heavens and the powers of heaven to be moved, we should not be affected because we rest, far above creatures, in the bosom of the Creator. Hence the Book of Wisdom says: "Therefore shall they receive the splendid crown, the beauteous diadem, from the hand of the Lord—for he shall shelter them with his right hand, and protect them with his arm. He shall take his zeal for armor and he shall arm creation to requite the enemy" (Wisdom 5:16-17).

Our first parents, following the example of the

fallen Angels, willed "to be as God." Yes, God himself wills that we be as he. Yet not without him, not outside him, nor opposed to him. He wills not that we should make ourselves as other gods to adore ourselves or be adored. He wills that we be as he, but in his bosom, at his heart. He wills it through himself, and in union with him as his own Divine Son, who is not another God, but one God with the Father. What therefore is the folly and crime of the sinner, who rejects the infinite goodness and mercy of God and sets up his judgment and will in opposition to him!

6. DIVINE GRACE IS THE PLEDGE OF FUTURE GLORY

"I will be as the Most High," was the aspiration of Lucifer when he looked upon the glory and beauty with which his Creator had adorned him, and because he wished to possess this glory independently and in defiance of God he was condemned. But we cannot give God greater praise and render thanks more pleasing to him than by confessing that by his divine grace he will make us similar to himself. Our Lord tells us: "Be perfect as your heavenly Father is perfect." Though these words are doubtless to be understood primarily of moral perfection, they may also be interpreted to mean that we shall partake of the other perfections of God. Accordingly, the poor man—destitute, forsaken, despised by all though he sees himself to be—has no reason to envy the rich man surrounded by friends. For if he is in a state of grace he has the Son of God for his friend, the Paraclete abides in him, and he is a sharer in the riches of the Eternal Father, for Christ has said: "The kingdom of God is within you."

But you will answer: "All these glories are hidden from me, and of what use is a treasure to me if I do not enjoy it?" True, it is kept from us during our mortal life—for, as St. John says: "We are now the sons of God, but it has not yet appeared what we shall be when we shall see God as he is." As long as the sight of God is withheld from us we cannot see the image of his Divine Nature in us. Divine grace is, so to speak, the dawn of the light of the Divine Sun, which, when it rises upon us in the everlasting day, will penetrate us with its glory and its warmth. Until then we must, in the words of the Apostle, walk by faith and not by sight, trusting in God's unfailing promises. St. Peter tells us, we: "Are guarded with God's power through faith; a birth to a salvation which stands ready to be revealed in the last days" (I Peter 1:5). And by him we have the lively hope of "a birth to an imperishable inheritance, incapable of fading or defilement, which is kept in heaven for you" (I Peter 1:4). In divine grace we have the pledge—yes, the root—of our future glorification in soul and body. If you still sigh in the servitude of the flesh, if you feel depressed by suffering and trials, sigh with the Apostle for your true home where the mercies of God will be revealed to you.

7. INFINITE DISTANCE BETWEEN GOD AND HUMAN BEINGS

Man, inasmuch as he is a reasonable being, bears some resemblance to God, but the distance between his nature and that of God is no less than infinite. God therefore can only by seen at an immeasurable distance. "Everyone beholds him afar off." Creatures only see, as it were, the hem of his garment, the reflex of his glory in his great and glorious creation, for as the Apostle says: "He alone has immortality and dwells in unapproachable light, whom no human being has ever seen or can see" (I Tim. 6:16). Even the cherubim cover their faces and fall prostrate before him in the deepest reverence. God himself alone can by his nature behold his being. Only the "only begotten Son who is in the bosom of the Father," and is of the same nature with him, beholds him face to face. Only the Holy Spirit, who is in God, penetrates and fathoms his innermost nature. To behold God, we must either be God or participate in the Divine Nature. Thus, the spiritual sight of man must become in a sense divine, and his soul partake of the Divine Nature, if he will see God face to face. The Holy Spirit effects this in us when by grace he makes us partake of the Divine Nature. For what else is the meaning of these words: "All of us, gazing on the Lord's glory with unveiled faces, are being transformed from glory to glory into his very image by the Lord who is the Spirit" (II Cor. 3:18). St. John teaches likewise: "We shall be like him, for we shall see him as he is" (I John 3:2). Our Lord also at the Last Supper addressed his Father thus: "I have given them the glory you gave me that they may be one, as we are one" (John 17:22). In heaven we shall, moreover, know God as he knows himself, and as he knows us. "Then I shall know," exclaims the Apostle, "even as I am known" (I Cor. 13:12). But it is impossible, as a holy doctor of the Church urges, that we should have a knowledge which is peculiar to the Divine Nature if we were not really made to participate in it, for the vision of God could not be communicated to us unless we were deified (Dionys. Areop., Vulg de eccl. hier., c. 1. 83). Truly we are forced to exclaim with St. Peter: "God has called us into his marvelous light."

Providence has implanted in our hearts a great thirst for knowledge and truth, but this knowledge and this truth can only be found in him—that is, by revelation, or the teaching of his Church. He himself introduces us into his admirable light. "In your light we shall see light," says the Psalmist. Only in his own light, and not in *our* light, can we see God.

If, then, we experience, in common with every child of Adam, an inexpressible desire for the perception of truth and the enjoyment of the beautiful, why do we not seek to satisfy it at its Source? That is, in God. The light of divine grace will introduce us to the light of God. In heaven he will manifest to us his own beauty, in the enjoyment of which he, with the Son and the Holy Spirit, is happy for ever and ever: that beauty which unites in itself all the possible and imaginable beauties of his works with all their wonderful diversity, that beauty which the Angels behold and can never tire of, and one ray of which is enough to intoxicate all created beings with joy unspeakable.

"You my glance seeks," we should say with the Psalmist, "your presence, O Lord, I seek" (Ps. 27:8). If we love him, in our measure and degree, as he loves us, then we shall know him as we are known.

"I cannot express, O my God," says St. Anselm, "how happy your elect will be. Certainly they will rejoice according to the measure of their love, and they will love after the measure of their knowledge. But how great will be their knowledge, and how great their love! Truly no eye has seen, nor ear heard, nor has it entered in this life into the heart of man, how much they will know, and love you in the world to come. I beg you, O God, that I may know you, love you, rejoice in you, and, if I cannot do so perfectly in this life, that I may at least progress from day to day until I arrive at this perfection. Let my knowledge of you progress here, and be perfect there. Let my love increase here, and become perfect there that my joy may be great in hope here and perfect in possession there. O Lord, you bid and counsel us to ask through your Son, and promise that our joy will be full. I beg you, then, O true and faithful God, grant that our joy may be complete. Meanwhile, may my soul consider it, my tongue speak of it, my heart love it. May my spirit hunger for it, my flesh thirst for it, my whole being desire it, until I enter into the joy of the Lord, who as the Triune God be blessed for ever. Amen" (Anselm, in Proslog., sub finem).

8. SANCTIFYING GRACE AS A SHARING IN THE TRANSCENDING HOLINESS OF GOD

Amidst all the glories which surround God in heaven, there is one which attracts the enraptured praise of the seraphim more than any other, and that is his sanctity: "Holy, holy, holy, Lord God of hosts," is their unceasing cry. Accordingly, we shall be perfect partakers of the Divine Nature only when, by the grace of the Holy Spirit, we participate in its sanctity. The Fathers of the Church identify this partaking of the Divine Nature with being holy as God is holy. They compare the sanctity of God with a great and potent fire which penetrates our imperfect nature, transforms and cleanses it from all dross and stain, so that our goodness becomes like to the Divine. "Even the princes and powers of heaven," says St. Basil, "are not by nature holy. The iron lying in the furnace does not lose the nature of iron, yet by its contact with the fire it becomes fiery itself and penetrated by the fire so that it assumes its heat and brilliancy. So the souls of Angels and of men have by their vision with God, the essentially Holy One, this sanctity implanted into their being, with this difference only: that the Holy Spirit is by nature holiness while their holiness is a participation of his sanctity" (Basil, Contra Eunom., b. iii).

This term, therefore, of sanctifying grace is one of deep significance. It not only implies that by divine grace we obtain forgiveness of sin, but still more that our soul is made an image of the divine goodness and sanctity. It further signifies that divine grace is irreconcilable with sin, and cannot exist in the same soul with it. If we commit a mortal sin, our natural faculties and light of reason are not thereby destroyed, but grace and its accompanying virtues instantly depart from our souls because grace, being of divine nature and origin, can coexist with sin as little as God himself. When divine grace, accordingly, has terminated in the light of glory, and has perfectly united our souls with God, and made them like to him, then we shall lose even the ability to commit sin. By its inherent divine virtue, we shall be as incapable of committing sin as God himself.

9. TRANSFORMATION IN CHRIST BY DIVINE GRACE

By divine grace, as we have seen, man receives a participation of the Divine Nature, is thus endowed with a new nature, and lays aside his former one. This

St. Paul describes as a transformation. "You are," he says, "transformed from glory to glory into his very image" (II Cor. 3:18), for by it we are created anew, and receive a new being of which our natures did not contain so much as a germ before. St. Cyril of Alexandria speaks of this recreation in the following terms: "If we have once taken leave of the life of the senses, is it not evident by this surrender of our former selves and union with the Holy Spirit that we are changed into a heavenly image, and transformed, to a certain extent, into another nature? We can then, with justice, be called, not men only, but children of God, having become participants in the Divine Nature" (In Joannem, I., II., c. 12, ad 27). What has been said of a transformation of one nature does not mean that our natural substance is destroyed, or absorbed in the Divine Substance, which would be a grave error. Yet it would not be sufficient to say that divine grace makes us new men in the sense in which a change of disposition or the acquirement of new habits makes us new men.

The change wrought by divine grace comes from God, not from the will or power of the creature. It is a miracle of the divine omnipotence which lifts us into a higher sphere, far above human limitations, and so transforms us that we are not only changed men, but we also appear as beings of a divine nature or kind.

The Fathers of the Church again make use of the illustration of the iron which is transformed by heat without changing its substance. This is one which lends itself perhaps more than any other to explain the change which takes place in our souls by means of divine grace. As the defects and imperfections of iron are burnt up and destroyed when it is plunged into a furnace, and yet its substance remains the same, in a similar manner, St. Cyril teaches, we do not put off the substance of our nature but only its lowliness and defects.

Elsewhere he compares it to a garment and says: "Those who are called by the faith of Christ to the sonship of God have deposed the lowliness of their own nature, and, glorified by the divine grace of God and adorned with it as with a precious garment, are raised to a supernatural dignity" (In Joannem, I. I. 14). We lose nothing by sanctifying grace that we have hitherto possessed, rather do we receive what was hitherto wanting to us according to the word of St. Paul, "We do not wish to be stripped naked but rather to have the heavenly dwelling envelop us, so that what is mortal may be absorbed by life" (II Cor. 5:4). The garment of divine grace is not only super-added to the immortal soul, as raiment is to the body, it likewise invests and penetrates the soul in the same way as the glow of fire penetrates the iron which is submitted to its heat.

By nature a man is a servant of God, by divine grace he is made his child. He ascends a step in the ladder of beings, is placed in a new relation to God, to his fellowmen and to corporal things, and enters a new sphere of life, one which is heavenly rather than earthly. Man in his natural state is composed of two natures—a corporal and a spiritual. Again, there are in him two men, an outward and inward man to whom the Apostle gives the name of "inner being and body" (II Cor. 4:16). Since we cannot serve both natures at the same time, we must subject the corporal to the spiritual. But as the flesh should serve the spirit, so should our spirit serve God and his divine grace, and as the spirit is superior to the flesh, so is divine grace superior to the spirit. If the spirit subjects itself to the flesh, it is drawn down to the level of the flesh and becomes carnal itself. However, if it gives itself up to grace, and is penetrated and moved by it, it becomes in a measure divine. "Who loves earth," says St. Augustine, "is of earth. Who loves God, what shall I say brethren? Not I, but the word of God will tell you. Who loves God becomes as God: 'I have said, you are gods' " (John 10:34).

In the same measure in which we cooperate with divine grace, and tend toward the Author of divine grace, the Father of light, we are filled with his light and glory and partake of his divine nature. Lest, however, we should forget as Lucifer and our first parents forgot that of ourselves we are nothing, and that we owe all we possess to the goodness of God, he has given us a powerful reminder in the "sting of our flesh," for our chastisement, our confusion and our wholesome humiliation. But even this knowledge of our weakness and the lowliness of our origin should not rob us of the sense of our heavenly dignity. For with the Apostle we may say: "And so I willingly boast of my weaknesses instead, that the power of Christ may rest upon me. Therefore I am content with weakness . . . for when I am powerless, it is then that I am strong" (II Cor. 12:1-10).

10. EVERY SUPERNATURAL ACTION MERITS AN INCREASE OF DIVINE GRACE

Divine grace enables the soul to raise itself far above its natural limitations, to behold God in his infinite nature, to possess and enjoy him. How could it do this if it did not contain something of the infinite power of God?

All created natures have a circumscribed and distinctly definite limit beyond which they cannot rise or increase without changing their nature. Divine grace alone knows no such restrictions, it is bound by no limits. Being a ray of the divine nature glorifying our immortal soul, it has its measure and end only in the infinity of God. It may increase daily and hourly and incessantly grow richer, greater and nobler, it never transgresses its appointed limits because it has none. It always remains divine grace and is always a participation of the Divine Nature, yet it always becomes more and more what it is destined to be. St. Thomas says that nothing is able to set limits to supernatural love (and the same may be said of divine grace), since it has its origin in the infinite power of God, and is itself nothing else but a participation in the sanctity of God" (Thom. 2, 2, qu. 24, a. 7). Certainly the vessel which receives it is narrow and limited, but divine grace extends the capacity of our nature, and every measure of grace received qualifies it for a still greater measure. Every degree of divine grace is a step leading to the next degree so that the farther one progresses the higher is our ascent.

Every degree of divine grace is in itself infinitely valuable, more precious than all created things in heaven and on earth and a treasure for which we should, with the Apostle, "count all things lost that we may gain Christ" and his divine grace. Every supernatural action performed in the state of grace, every moment utilized and made to bear fruit, merits another increase of divine grace from God. It rests only with man to double this grace again in a short time, and the greater this increase of grace the greater also the merit of our works.

Divine grace gives an immense scope to our aims and desires, and yet leaves them the freest possible play. We have only to desire it in order to obtain it, and only to love its donor to receive it. By this ardent desire for divine grace and of the love of our heavenly Father, we acquire all good gifts, and that according to the measure of our love and desire. Why do we not manifest a holy eagerness to possess ourselves of these treasures and like St. Paul, forgetting the things that are behind, "push on to what is ahead. My entire attention is on the finish line as I run toward the prize to which God calls me—life on high in Christ Jesus" (Phil. 3:13-14). Oh that we were as eager to lay up treasures in heaven as we are to add to our possessions here below! The desire to acquire money is a source of endless disquietude, but a holy thirst for divine grace leads us to an eternal rest in God, who will satisfy us the more in proportion to the greater love and desire we have had for him on earth. Divine grace, moreover, permits us to enjoy our possessions on the way to that end, because at every step we make in our upward ascent we experience more and more how sweet is the Lord to those who serve him and are of a right heart.

11. THE SUBLIME INTERCHANGE OF HEAVENLY GIFTS IN THE INCARNATION

The two great mysteries of the Christian faith—the Incarnation of the Word and the divine maternity of Mary—reveal the greatness of the treasures of divine grace in a still stronger light, for in a very real sense it may be fitly compared with them.

"Which is the more adorable mystery," says St.

Peter Chrysologus, "that God gave himself to the earth, or that he gives you to heaven? That he himself enters into such intimate union with our flesh, or that he introduces us to companionship with the Godhead? That he is born like us to servitude, or that he generates us as his freeborn children? That he adopts our poverty, or that he makes us his heirs and the coheirs of his only begotten Son? Certainly, it is more astounding and worthy of praise that earth should be transferred to heaven, man should be transformed by the Deity and the rank condition of slavery receive the rights of dominion" (Homil. 67). Again, the same writer says: "So great is the Divine condescension toward us that the creature knows not which to admire more, that God has descended to our servitude, or that he has transported us to the Divine dignity" (Ibid., 72).

Therefore the Church makes the priest say daily in the Mass, "O God, let us partake of his Divinity, who has deigned to partake of our humanity" and this equalization, this balance between the humiliation of God and the elevation of man by divine grace has so deep a reason that the holy Fathers teach that the Son of God was made man on account of divine grace to elevate us by this same grace. "God was made man that man might be made God," says St. Augustine, "the Son of God was made the son of man that the children of man might be made children of God" (Aug., Siren., 13). And this doctrine is contained in the words of the Apostle: "God sent forth his Son born of a woman . . . so that we might receive our status as adopted sons" (Gal. 4:4). St. Fulgentius gives a beautiful explanation of this passage: "God was born of man that man might be born of God. The first birth of Christ as the Son of God was of God, the second of man. Our first birth is of man, our second of God. And because God to be born of woman adopted the reality of the flesh, he has given us at our regeneration in Baptism the spirit of sonship. What Christ was not by nature at his first birth, that he was made at his second birth by grace, so that we might also be made by the grace of the second birth what we were not by nature of the first. God, however, has brought us divine grace when he was born of man. We, on the other hand, receive divine grace gratuitously, that by the gift of the Incarnate God we might partake of the divine nature" (Ep. 17, sive lib. ad Petr., cap. 7, nn. 14, 16). If, then, the condescension of God in his Incarnation appears to us inconceivably great—as great as is the infinite distance between God and the creature—must not the elevation of man to God, which is its cause and reason, likewise astound us almost in the same measure and degree?

The humanity of Christ may be considered not only in its personal union with the Son of God, but also in regard to the qualities which it received on account of its divine dignity, and here again the greatness of grace is made manifest. God in all his wisdom and power could give the human soul of his Son no more worthy condition than that which our immortal soul receives by divine grace, for it is the most sublime that can be found in a creature. One distinction only is there between the soul of Christ and our own. The soul of the Son of God has every claim and right to divine grace, merits it instead of receiving it as a gratuitous gift, it likewise receives grace directly and in exceeding abundance, and can in no wise lose it. Our soul receives divine grace as a gratuitous gift through Christ, in a limited measure and may easily lose it by sin.

Again, the divine dignity which the sacred human-ity of Christ receives through the personal union with the Eternal Word is reflected upon all the members of humankind. As that Sacred Humanity was made the true Body of Christ, so all regenerated mankind was made the Mystical Body of Christ. Christ is indeed the Head, and we are his members. Inasmuch as we are one with him, we enjoy already, apart from divine grace, a certain supernatural dignity, and as he had a right to grace, so we acquire a right to it through him. By him mankind appropriates divine grace, and pos-sesses it as something which is due to it on account of its Head. Christ is the heavenly Vine permeated by the fullness of divine life, and we are the branches into which this life is diffused.

"O Christian soul," St. Leo exclaims, "acknowl-edge your dignity, know that as a Christian you sur-pass the Angels not only in nature, but also in divine grace! For the Angels are kindred to God by one tie only, because they partake of this Divine Nature. You, however, in a twofold manner, because God has also adopted your nature. If these pure and holy spirits were capable of envy, they would envy us because God has taken upon himself the nature, not of Angels or Archangels, but of the seed of Abraham" (Heb. 2:16).

"Very foolish," says the venerable monk, Job, "are they who would rather be Angels than men." For al-though the Angels are not subject to tribulations and death, yet they have not the Son of God for their Brother, nor have they the supreme consolation and honor of uniting and sharing even by this means, their labors and sorrows with him.

By Holy Baptism we are incorporated into the Mystical Body of Christ and in token of this union, and as a pledge of it, we receive the sacramental character by which we are made Christ's and he becomes ours. Moreover, we are, as it were, Christ himself—"Totus Christus," as St. Augustine calls us, inasmuch as we, the Body, and Christ the Head, form a whole. The character is indelible in our immortal soul, and gives us, as long as we live, a right to the divine grace of God, because the Body of Christ must also be filled by Christ's life of glory. But this right belongs to us only as long as we fear him and keep his command- ments, "for this is all man."

12. THE MYSTERIES OF THE INCARNATION AND THE DIVINE MOTHERHOOD OF MARY

In the mystery of the Incarnation, a human *nature* only is elevated to a divine dignity. The divine ma- ternity, however, is a supernatural dignity which was communicated to a human *person:* it is therefore more easily compared with the dignity granted to us by grace. The first truth we have to keep in mind is that in Mary divine grace cannot be separated from her divine maternity. This is the meaning of the dogma of the Immaculate Conception—namely, that it cannot be supposed that the Mother of God was even for one moment despoiled of his divine grace. "God is inseparably united with her," is an axiom laid down by the holy Bishop and martyr Methodius in the third century. Because she communicated her human nature of the Son of God, she has a right as none other has ever had to the participation in his divine nature by grace. As Mother she forms one person, as it were, with her Son. His rights are her rights, his gifts hers, his sanctity her sanctity. She is the woman seen by St. John in his revelations "clothed with the sun, with the moon under her feet" (Rev. 12:1). The divine grace, therefore, that filled her soul has this prerogative above that of all other creatures, that it is especially due to her as the grace of her Divine Son is due to him. As it is said of her Son that he is full of grace and truth, so she is called by the Angel, not only blessed with divine grace, but full of divine grace. As Christ is the only begotten Son of the Father, so is Mary his firstborn daughter. But apart from this august union, and considering the maternal dignity of Mary alone, we may safety assert that divine grace is a greater gift, and confers a higher dignity than that holy office itself. As Mother of God according to the flesh, Mary ranks high above all creatures, but she would rather be a daughter of God by divine grace than the Mother of God by nature. She well knows that, notwithstanding the incomparable filial love which Jesus bears for her, he would nevertheless love another soul more if this soul were richer in divine grace.

It was this great truth which Christ intimated to his disciples when they came to tell him his Mother awaited him. " 'Who is my mother? Who are my brothers?' Then, extending his hand toward his disciples, he said, 'There are my mother and my brothers. Whoever does the will of my heavenly Father is brother and sister and mother to me' " (Matt. 12:48-50). And again when in answer to the woman who cried out, "Blest is the womb that bore you and the breasts that nursed you!" He replied, "Rather, blest are they who hear the word of God and keep 't" (Luke 11:27-28).

By these words our Lord intends us to understand

that his Mother was blessed and worthy of him for the reason that she performed the will of his Father in the most perfect manner, and if another could have exceeded her in this respect he would honor her more than he did his own ever-blessed Mother.

As Mother of our Savior in the flesh, she gave birth to him according to the flesh. However, by receiving the Word of God into her immortal soul she conceived and brought forth her Son spiritually, was clothed with the splendor of his divine nature, and thus entered into a heavenly relationship with him. Thus, St. Augustine says: "The maternity would have profited the Virgin nothing if she had not borne Christ still more happily in the spirit than she bore him in the flesh." By divine grace we are made to resemble in a marvelous manner the Mother of God, since we imitate in ourselves the maternity of Mary by the reception of divine grace. The same Holy Spirit that descended into the bosom of Mary to confer on her a holy fertility descends also into our immortal soul to generate in a spiritual manner the Son of God. As the Blessed Virgin, by lending a willing ear to the Angel and fulfilling the will of God, was made the Mother of the Son in the flesh and in the spirit, so must we give birth spiritually to the Son of God by faithfully receiving the Word of God and corresponding to his divine grace and his commands. Penetrated with the greatness of God's mercies to us, should we not, then, join in Mary's great hymn of thanksgiving: "My being proclaims the greatness of the Lord, my spirit finds joy in God my savior, . . . God who is mighty has done great things for me" (Luke 1:46-47, 49).

Mary is not our Mother according to our human nature, as this we received from Eve, and not from

Mary. She is our Mother insofar as we are the brethren of her divine Son, and are the living members of his Mystical Body. She is our Mother according to divine grace by which we have received a new heavenly nature and partake of the nature of her Son. Therefore, as God alone can be our Father by divine grace, so our Mother by divine grace can be no other than the Mother of God.

How highly should we value this privilege, and how careful should we be lest by the loss of divine grace we go over from her to her enemy and the enemy of her adorable Son!

13. DIVINE GRACE IS THE PEARL OF GREAT PRICE

One thing remains to be said to prove the ineffable value of divine grace in the sight of God, and that is the infinite value of the price God himself paid for it. What more could he have done than he has accomplished to procure it for us? For in purchasing divine grace for mankind he has not spared his only begotten Son.

Even the human life of the Son of God is a divine life, on account of the infinite dignity of his person, and can only by sacrificed for the sake of another divine life. Neither heaven nor earth, with all the splendor and countless number of beings they contain, was worthy to be bought and saved by the life of the Son of God or even by a tear or a drop of his blood. And yet theologians say that the Son of God would not have become man and died in vain should he have acquired grace for only one immortal soul. By sacrificing his life for us the Son of God would have us understand that by so doing he has purchased for us the life of children of God, and that the divine grace that adorns our immortal soul possesses a value as infinitely great as that of his own precious blood. For if his corporeal life is of infinite dignity, because it belongs to a divine person, the life of grace is of equal value, because it makes us partakers of the divine nature.

Man by the sins of his first parents lost the grace which God in his infinite love had originally bestowed upon him. In order to recover it for him, God, with equal or even greater love, himself became man to restore to mankind the dignity they had forfeited and to bring them back to his paternal bosom. Behold, the Son of man descends from the highest heavens and is made flesh, suffers the torments of the Passion, and dies on the Cross. All this he undergoes for love of us, and to acquire that divine grace which the world esteems so lightly. Nor did he believe he purchased it too dearly even at such a price. If, then, the Son of God, who in his unspeakable wisdom estimates all things according to their true value, would purchase divine grace so dearly for us, how grieved we should be to lose it! Or, rather, should we not look upon such a loss as the greatest misfortune which could possibly befall us?

It did not satisfy Christ merely to take upon himself our nature and die for us, but for thirty-three years he labored and suffered for us. All his actions had an infinite value. Accordingly, by one drop of his precious blood, one action of his, he might have merited divine grace again for us. But, to make us fully aware of the infinite value of divine grace, he would show that even a God-man could not do and suffer too much for it. Therefore he suffered all that man could suffer: he fasted forty days, he endured his agony in the garden, the scourging at the pillar, the torments of the Cross in order to raise us to the throne of divine grace and fill us with divine life. In the light of our Savior's toils and anguish should we not understand that all sacrifices we are called upon to make for the sake of divine grace are nothing compared to its infinite value? If we had to suffer all that Christ suffered and to endure the torments of hell, we could not merit the least degree of grace. What limit should there be, accordingly, to our gratitude to him for having earned for us what we could not possibly have earned for ourselves and what is of such priceless value to us?

Nor is this all that Christ has done for us to propagate the blessings of divine grace. At the Last Supper he instituted a sacrifice and sacrament which contains nothing less than his own precious Body and Blood, which are the wellsprings of all grace. Not satisfied with being born for us in the stable of Bethlehem, he comes again daily in ten thousand churches all over the world, at the word of the priest to give himself to all who ask to receive him. His love induces him to expose himself to the insults of the irreligious who receive him sacrilegiously and the neglect of the indifferent and lukewarm. In this way he again proves that there is no sacrifice he is not willing to make to increase divine grace in the immortal souls of the children of men. The words of the Apostle put these great truths before us in the most forcible terms: "You are not your own. You have been purchased, and at a price. So glorify God in your body" (I Cor. 6-19-20).

To conclude, divine grace is held in such high regard by God that he would rather that every evil should fall upon man, and that the world should be thrown into confusion than permit the loss of divine grace. Thus, have we not all heard or read in history of fearful epidemics, of wars and earthquakes which have destroyed flourishing communities and converted smiling lands into deserts? Of persecutions waged against the just in which the sinner appears to triumph? All these evils, for which many men blame Divine Providence, are permitted by God because temporal misfortunes are as nothing to him compared to the loss of grace which these trials are intended to convey to man, or which is preserved to him by means of them. Divine grace is the pearl of great price and, like the man in the parable, we should willingly part with all we possess, and even submit to every earthly trial which can befall us, rather than part with it.

II

The Sublime Union with God to Which We Are Introduced Through Divine Grace

1. **DIVINE GRACE EFFECTS SUBLIME UNION OF IMMORTAL SOUL WITH GOD**

2. **INDWELLING OF THE MOST BLESSED TRINITY IN IMMORTAL SOUL**

3. **CHILDREN OF GOD BY VIRTUE OF DIVINE GRACE**

4. **GOD'S CREATURES ARE CALLED TO LIVES OF SPIRITUAL PERFECTION**

5. **IN HOLY COMMUNION JESUS ENRICHES IMMORTAL SOULS WITH DIVINE GRACES**

6. **LIBERTY AND EQUALITY BESTOWED UPON MERE MORTALS BY DIVINE GRACE**

7. **BEAUTY OF IMMORTAL SOUL IS EMBELLISHED BY DIVINE GRACE**

8. **OUR INCORPORATION WITH JESUS BY DIVINE GRACE**

The Sublime Union with God
to Which We Are Introduced
Through Divine Grace

1. DIVINE GRACE EFFECTS SUBLIME UNION OF IMMORTAL SOUL WITH GOD

In the preceding chapter we have seen how sanctifying grace makes us partakers of the divine nature. We shall now consider the intimate union which is thereby effected between the immortal soul and God.

In the words of Scripture and the Fathers of the Church, the Holy Spirit is generally designated as that Person with whom we are specially united by divine grace. For the Holy Spirit as the Third Person of the Blessed Trinity, stands, as it were, on the boundary of the Blessed Trinity, therefore the union of God with the creature is primarily attributed to him. He is also the personal representative of the Divine Love from which he proceeds. Since therefore the union of God with the creature is effected by his love, and our union with God in this life consists principally in our love for him, it is evident why the Holy Spirit represents the Blessed Trinity. The Holy Spirit, accordingly, comes to us with divine grace, he gives us himself and really and essentially dwells in us in an unspeakably intimate manner by this same divine grace.

The Holy Spirit it is who, in the words of the Apostle, transforms us into his very image by the Lord who is the Spirit" (II Cor. 3:18). In this he does not act like the sun, which lights up the earth with its rays from a distance, because as God he must be present wherever he acts. He illuminates our immortal soul like a light that is placed within a crystal globe. Or, to use another figure, he is the seal by which God impresses upon our immortal soul the image of his holiness and divine nature. In giving us his divine grace the Holy Spirit gives us himself, as St. Paul says: "The love of God has been poured out in our hearts through the Holy Spirit who has been given to us" (Rom. 5:5).

"By sanctifying grace," we learn from St. Thomas, "the rational creature is thus perfected, that it may not only use with liberty the created good, but that it may also enjoy the uncreated good. Therefore, the invisible sending of the Holy Spirit takes place in the gift of sanctifying grace at the same time that the divine Person is given us" (I. p. 9, q. 33, art. 2).

By divine grace, therefore, we are not only qualified to know, love, and enjoy God from afar mediately, by the beauty and goodness of his creatures, but to possess him immediately in his substance. As theologians for the most part teach, with regard to the beatific vision, that it cannot be imagined without a true and exceedingly intimate presence of God in our immortal soul, so we must likewise hold that we cannot love God in this life with a supernatural love unless he is intimately united to us and present in our immortal soul.

In a twofold manner, then, and from a twofold cause we are truly and really united to the Holy Spirit by grace. First, as the Author of divine grace, he comes to us with grace and unites himself with us, and again divine grace conducts us to him and unites us with him. The Holy Spirit and the Divinity itself is present also in all natural things. In human beings he is present as their Creator only without whom they cannot exist, but in souls possessed of divine grace he is present as their Sanctifier. He gives himself to them and discloses to them the depths of his own Being. He is in them in the same way as God the Father is in his only begotten Son.

Although the Holy Spirit dwells in the whole created nature as in a vast temple, as the Scriptures say of him, "The Spirit of the Lord has filled the whole world," yet he dwells in a special manner in the soul adorned by divine grace. Suarez says, "If God should cease to be present in other creatures, he would not cease to be in the immortal souls that are in a state of grace, any more than he would thereby separate himself from the Sacred Humanity of Christ which is united with him in one person. Therefore, if all creation is his temple, the immortal soul is his altar; if that is his house, this is his innermost chamber. . . . Shall I say even more? In the soul which is in a state of grace the Holy Spirit is as intimately present as the immortal soul is present in the heart, of which it is the principle of life and action" (Suarez, de Tri., lib. 12, p. 5).

The Holy Spirit does not come to us as a passing guest. Our Savior prayed for us to the Father that he might send us the Paraclete, the Spirit of Truth, to abide with us forever. Never will he leave us unless we ourselves expel him from our hearts. If Zaccheus called himelf blessed because he received for a short time the Son of God under his roof, how much more should we rejoice at the intimate presence of the Holy Spirit of God, who comes to take possession of our souls to abide there for ever!

The Holy Spirt brings with him a great treasure, which is himself, and he is the pledge of an eternal one. For St. Paul says: "He is the pledge of our inheritance" (Eph. 1:14). As this inheritance is none other than God himself, the pledge for it can be no other than God. For only a divine pledge can secure us a divine inheritance, and give us a foretaste of the enjoyment of God. Oh, how insensible are we of the value of this treasure and of the living hope this pledge gives us! The Spirit of divine charity can only be perceived and enjoyed in the measure in which we receive his love. The more we love him, the nearer he approaches us and we experience his heavenly sweetness, the stronger will our desire grow to possess one day, not only the pledge, but the whole treasure of God himself. But if we do not cultivate this love in us, then we ourselves are at fault if we do not experience the presence of the Holy Spirit in our soul, and we even run the risk of losing it.

The Holy Spirit comes to us for our own good and our happiness, but at the same time he comes as our Lord and God to take possession of our immortal soul. "You must know," says the Apostle, "that your body is a temple of the Holy Spirit, who is within— the Spirit you have received from God. You are not your own" (I Cor. 6:19). What a crime it would be to desecrate his dwelling place! "If any man violate the temple of God," again we read, "him shall God destroy. For the temple of God is holy, which you are."

The members of our body are members of Christ, by whom we have received the Holy Spirit, therefore they are his instruments and dedicated to his service and glory. Thus the Apostle tells us: "It is God's will that you grow in holiness" (I Thess., 4:3). And again: "Do not, therefore, let sin rule your mortal body and make you obey its lusts; no more shall you offer the members of your body to sin as weapons for evil. Rather offer yourselves . . . as weapons for justice" (Rom. 6:12-13).

The Son of God became incarnate once only, for man's redemption, and the Angels of God, and man, have never ceased marveling at his mercy and condescension. He dwelt also in one country only and among one people. The Holy Spirit, however, who is equal to the Father and the Son, comes to each one of us, enters our soul, makes it his dwelling place: should we not, therefore, do our utmost to welcome this Divine Guest by manifesting our love and gratitude to him?

Our Savior gave the Holy Spirit twice to his Apostles: immediately after his Resurrection, and on Pentecost Day. St. Augustine reasons from this that, being the Spirit of Love, the Holy Spirit was to confer on them thereby a double love—for God and their neighbor (August., de Tri., lib. 15, cap. 26). Oh, how few realize that their neighbors are temples of the Holy Spirit and love and reverence them as such! Were we as enlightened as the Saints, we should kneel before the sick and helpless and willingly render them the most humiliating services, perceiving that we are rendering them to him who dwells in them. For it is by love for our neighbor that we make our own souls pleasing to God. "If anyone says, 'My love is fixed on God,' yet hates his brother, he is a liar. One who has no love for the brother he has seen cannot love the God he has not seen" (I John 4:20).

2. INDWELLING OF THE MOST BLESSED TRINITY IN IMMORTAL SOUL

The beloved disciple says, "The way we know we remain in him and he in us is that he has given us of his Spirit" (I John 4:13). The Three Persons of the Blessed Trinity being inseparably united with one another on account of the unity of their essence which means that when one is present the two others must also be present. Thus, our Lord says: "Anyone who loves me will be true to my word, and my Father will love him; we will come to him and make our dwelling place with him" (John 14:23).

St. Augustine explains in what sense we may in the Pater Noster address the words "who art in heaven" to God the Father. He says that the word "heaven" signifies the just on earth and the Angels above, in whom, as in a magnificent royal palace, God the Father dwells with the Son and the Holy Spirit. God always follows directly his divine grace. Accordingly, whoever receives it, receives into his immortal soul the Triune God, an incomparably greater favor than Abraham received when he visited him in his tent under the guise of three strangers. Must we not exclaim with holy Job: "What is man, that you make much of him, or pay him any heed?" (Job 7:17). Who can describe how loving the intercourse is between the devout soul and God, how he reveals his innermost nature to her, makes known his holy mysteries to such a soul and infuses into her a peace which transcends all understanding?

If the Blessed Trinity is present within us, this presence canot be without fruit. God is a living God and the Holy Spirit is the breath of divine life. He must, then, dwell in us as the soul of our immortal soul, and inspire it with a new life.

Our immortal soul has, certainly, its own life, but this life is scarcely a shadow of the divine life. It is so weak and limited that the soul endowed with it alone is rather to be called dead than alive when compared with God. Therefore by conferring the Holy Spirit upon us God may be said to breathe with exceeding goodness and kindness his divine life into our life, he thus converts its natural life into a divine and supernatural one. He may be said to plant a germ within us, which he irrigates with that living water of which he spoke to the Samaritan woman, when he told her it would become in her a fountain of water springing up into life everlasting.

Life in itself is so precious that every living being, be it ever so humble, is worth far more than all, even the greatest and most beautiful things which are inanimate. The natural life of the immortal soul is exceedingly precious, more so than the life of all other things on earth. But the sphere of this activity is very limited, as the immortal soul by its natural powers can directly comprehend and enjoy only natural things. Divine grace amplifies and elevates this sphere immeasurably. It qualifies the immortal soul to know God immediately in his glory and to receive within itself the highest good, and enjoy it as God himself enjoys it. Divine grace gives the soul a life infinitely superior to all natural life, a divine life full of unspeakable power and happiness.

Oh, that we esteemed this heavenly life of the immortal soul at least as much as the short and miserable life of the body, which is in reality a lingering death, and which every passing hour brings nearer its dissolution! Whereas our immortal soul by the divine grace of the Holy Spirit contains the germs of an eternal life. For, as St. Paul says, "Our inner being is renewed each day even though our body is being destroyed at the same time" (II Cor. 4:16), and this because "If the Spirit of him who raised Jesus from the dead dwells in you, then he who raised Christ from the dead will bring your mortal bodies to life also through his Spirit dwelling in you" (Rom. 8:11).

3. CHILDREN OF GOD BY VIRTUE OF DIVINE GRACE

"Whosoever are led by the Spirit of God, they are the sons of God," says St. Paul. Again, he tells us: "The proof that you are sons is the fact that God has sent forth into our hearts the spirit of his Son which cries out 'Abba!' (Father!)" (Gal. 4:6). "The Spirit himself gives witness with our spirit that we are children of God. But if we are children, we are heirs as well: heirs of God, heirs with Christ" (Rom. 8:16-17). Can anything show so clearly the glory of divine grace as the fact that it makes us children of God? Or could anything excite our love of God more than his adoption of us as his children? "See what love the Father has bestowed on us in letting us be called children of God! Yet that is what we are" (I John 3:1).

The words "Our Father who art in heaven" should be a revelation of the goodness of God to us, but we repeat these words so mechanically that it is as if they had no meaning for us. St. Peter Chrysologus in his instructions to his catechumens tells them to pause and tremble at the thought of the mighty condescension of God, that whereas they were sinners and slaves, subject to frailty and every vice, he bade them call him Father. He quotes the great prophet who, "having found the Lord had become his Father, cried out: 'I have considered your works, and have trembled.' Not because he contemplated the world and the harmony of its various elements, but because he beheld the work of divine tenderness in himself, therefore he was seized with wondering admiration and fear" (Peter Chrysol., Hom. 68).

By nature we are not, strictly speaking, children of God but only his servants and bondsmen, the least and humblest of all. Like the Angels—but in our nature far below them—we are creatures and the work of his hands. With all our likeness to him on the part of our rational soul, which is his image, we are not God's kindred, we are not begotten by him, neither have we received his divine nature. Only the Eternal and Uncreated Word is in a strict sense the Son of God. He alone is begotten of the Father, and proceeds from him as Light of Light, God of God, himself one God with the Father from all eternity. How can this creature, then, presume to call its Creator, the King of heaven and earth, Father? How can mortal man approach with confidence him before whom the seraphim prostrate in deepest reverence and veil their faces? To this there is the all-sufficient answer: What is impossible with men is possible to God. What we cannot claim as a right is gratuitously granted us by our infinitely loving and merciful God.

The Son of God undertook this great work of acquiring the life of children of God for us by the shedding of his blood. He was made flesh in order to "give to as many as received him the power to be made the sons of God." He was made our Brother in the flesh to make us his brethren in his divine glory. He looks upon it as an honor, not to be the "only begotten," but "the first-born among many brethren." Therefore, too, he is the first to call his Father ours, as well as his: "I ascend to my Father and to your Father." At the Last Supper his prayer for us is that we may be all one in him, as he is one with the Father. What return can we make for so much love? St. Peter Chrysologus makes this beautiful answer: "Return to God, by whom you are so well loved; devote yourself entirely to his honor, who for your sake exposed himself to the greatest dishonor, and acknowledge him as Father, whom you know and feel by his love for you to be your Parent."

4. GOD'S CREATURES ARE CALLED TO LIVES OF SPIRITUAL PERFECTION

God, in bestowing his divine grace upon us, imparts at the same time a goodness and supernatural beauty whereby we receive the fruit of this favor, and remain worthy of it. He, thus, not only loves us in and through his Son, as his children, but he really impresses upon us the image of his Son, and makes us resemble him that we may be truly his children. "Those whom he foreknew he predestined to share the image of his Son, that the Son might be the first-born of many brothers" (Rom. 8:29). He wills that we put on his only begotten Son, that we receive the impress of his features upon us and that we be clothed with his divine life. This he accomplishes when he receives us into his paternal bosom, and by the Holy Spirit gives birth to us in the waters of regeneration.

"Flesh begets flesh, Spirit begets spirit" (John 3:6), said our Savior to Nicodemus. It must be born again of water and the Holy Spirit in order to become spiritual and be raised to a spiritual life. Accordingly, St. James says: "Every worthwhile gift, every genuine benefit comes from above, descending from the Father of the heavenly luminaries. . . . He wills to bring us to birth with a word spoken in truth" (Jas. 1:17-18). We have a nature infinitely different from the divine, and, as St. Athanasius tells us, we are first created and afterwards generated of God, while the Son receives his being solely by this generation and has the same substance as the Father. Nevertheless, our relation as children of God to our heavenly Father is incomparably more intimate than that of adopted children to their parent. For we are generated and born of him in a similar manner to his own Son, since we receive the communication of his divine nature and life and are filled and animated by his Spirit. St. Peter therefore teaches: "Praised be the God and Father of our Lord Jesus Christ, he who in his great mercy gave us a new birth; a birth unto hope . . . a birth to an imperishable inheritance, incapable of fading or defilement, which is kept in heaven for you" (I Peter 1:3-4). Those whom God adopts he makes new men, he forms them after his own image and that of his Son, he seals them with his own Holy Spirit as the seal of their dignity and the pledge of their inheritance.

"Great is the mystery of this divine grace," says St. Leo, "and this gift which exceeds all gifts—namely, that God should call man son, and man should call

God Father. By these names we feel, and learn, what sentiments should correspond with such sublimity. For if among men it redounds to their glory that the splendor of ancestry should be reflected by its posterity, is it not far more glorious that those born of God should exhibit the image of their Father? As the Lord himself says: 'Let your light so shine before men, that seeing your good works they may glorify your Father who is in heaven'" (Serm. 6, de nativ. Dom.).

Again, the Son of God reminds us of our sublime destiny in the words: "Be you perfect as your heavenly Father is perfect." Because we are children of God, we must not be satisfied by leading a life of natural goodness, but, conscious of our high dignity we must seek to imitate our good and merciful God himself. Accordingly, St. Augustine, drawing a parallel between Alexander the Great and ourselves, remarks that if the delusion he possessed, that he was a descendant of the gods, led him to perform great and heroic actions, how much more should we, who by God's divine grace belong in truth to a heavenly and divine race, direct all our faculties to be like God, to seek him, and labor and suffer in his service!

If we are really children of God, then he will indeed be with us, and, "If God is for us, who can be against us? Who will separate us from the love of Christ? Trial, or distress, or persecution, or hunger or nakedness, or danger, or the sword? Yet in all this we are more than conquerors because of him who has loved us" (Rom. 8:31, 35, 37).

We must consider ourselves as pilgrims upon earth, journeying toward our heavenly country, and our life therefore should be conformable to the one to which we are destined. Far from attaching our hearts to the things of this world, and seeking our happiness in it, we should rather sigh and lament that our "sojourning is prolonged," and that we are not in our true home.

Let us also as St. Leo bids us, "put off the old Adam with his works, and, being made partakers of the generation of Christ, let us renounce the works of the flesh. Recognize your dignity, and as participant of the divine nature beware of returning to your former lowliness. . . . By the sacrament of Baptism you have been made a temple of the Holy Spirit, take care not to drive away so great a Guest by evil works, because the price of your purchase is the blood of Christ, and he will judge you in justice who has redeemed you in mercy" (Serm. I, de nativ. Dom., in fine).

5. IN HOLY COMMUNION JESUS ENRICHES IMMORTAL SOULS WITH DIVINE GRACES

"God, who has given himself to us as a Father, who has adopted us as his children, who has made us the heirs of his possessions, distinguished us with his Name, honored us with his glory and his kingdom, wills also that we ask of him our daily bread. But what bread is this? The heavenly Father can demand of his children to ask only a heavenly Bread, and this Bread is the Son of God, who says of himself: 'I am the Living Bread,' which laid upon the altars is daily offered to the faithful as a heavenly food" (Peter Chrysol., Hom. 67). The first duty of a parent is the nourishment of his children. But what mortal mind can comprehend the liberality of your love towards your children, O God? Oh love that no mother could have imagined! Oh more than paternal heart of my God!

Truly we can say with your prophet: "We have been nursed at the breast of Kings." But it was naturally becoming that, God being greater than man, the food prepared for his children should correspond with the greatness of their heavenly Father. Therefore God would place no limits to his love, he would pour out all the treasures of his omnipotence, and give his children the most precious of these treasures for their eternal banquet which is himself. For what is the good thing, and what is his beautiful thing, but "the wheat of the chosen ones, and the wine which makes virgins"?

But if this nourishment is so precious, we may judge from it the value of the life of divine grace which is maintained by it and the greatness of that dignity that merits it. If our body receives the Blood of Christ, is not that a sign that our soul, too, in regeneration is filled through divine grace with a divine life and possesses a divine nobility? If our body is united to the substance of the Body of Christ, is not this a pledge that by divine grace we have been made partakers of divine nature? Oh, if we had a lively faith, how highly we should esteem the life of grace which is worthy of such food! and with what loving desire we should approach this heavenly banquet which makes us partakers of the divine nature and fills us with divine life. But our admiration for this nourishment of the children of God, and for divine grace which is the object of it, will increase when we consider in what manner it is prepared for us. The entire substance of bread and the entire substance of wine are changed after consecration into the Body and Blood of the Son of God. Is this not a sign that our nature, in receiving this food and drink, is by divine grace entirely transformed? As the natural bread is by a miracle made a heavenly Bread, so divine grace coming to us in this sacrament converts our earthly nature into a heavenly one, and without destroying its substance makes it participate in the divine nature. It is true that this change is not visible to our senses, but neither does Transubstantiation affect the outward form of the bread and wine. Exteriorly the children of God are as other men, subject to the same trials and diseases, but as the Apostle says, "the outward man is corrupted, yet the inward man is renewed day by day." They are transformed by the Spirit of God, until hereafter their mortal life is changed into a glorious and immortal one.

The Body and Blood of his Son is, yet, not the greatest food which the heavenly Father gives to his children. In the Holy Sacrament the Son of God gives himself directly in his Sacred Humanity, because we are yet too immature, too small, to be able to comprehend him in his divinity. Here he gives himself, as it were, as the milk, there as the Bread of Eternal Life. "For as the mother," says St. Augustine, "prepares in her maternal breast, as milk, the bread which the infant cannot eat yet at the table of its father, so that the infant receiving it may become stronger and grow bigger, so the Word of God, who, with his Father in heaven, is the Bread of the elect, has descended to us on earth, and made himself small that he may be taken as milk by the new-born children of his Father. The Holy Sacrament of the Altar, therefore, though truly divine, is only a foretaste of, and a preparation for, that food with which God the Father will nourish us in heaven. There we shall enjoy the Son of God in his glory, there we shall be strengthened by the power of his divine nature, there we shall be nourished by the light of his glory and shall drink in the flood of his love and delight" (In Ps. XXX; cf. in Ps. cxix).

St. Francis de Sales has explained this sublime mystery very beautifully. "You alone, O God," he exclaims, "can enable us to see and feel the happiness and joy of the human understanding, when, receiving in itself, not the image, but the real presence and essence of the essential truth and divine majesty. It will see itself united for eternity to its End and Object. We shall then be nourished by the substance of God himself entering our souls through the medium of our understanding.

"The tender love of God toward us is almost incredible. Just as an affectionate mother makes use of no foreign means to communicate her substance to her child, but feeds him in it and by it, so our heavenly Parent does not confine himself to conveying an abstract idea of his divinity to our understanding, but by an excess of love he represents himself to the mind without the assistance of any image. In this way, it may be thereby seen and understood in itself that thereby this Divinity and Eternal Essence should become at once the object contemplated by the understanding and the medium by which it is contemplated. We shall then fully enjoy the accomplishment of these promises of God: 'Behold, I will bring upon her as it were a river of peace . . . you shall be carried at the breasts, and upon the knees they shall caress you. As one whom the mother caresses I will comfort you.' This is the boundless, the eternal happiness to which we aspire, and of which we have received the promise and pledge in the Holy Eucharist, the perpetual banquet of Divine grace. . . . There is, however, one difference: for the first favor, though real, is hidden under the veil of the sacramental species, whereas in heaven God will communicate himself to us in unclouded splendor, and we shall behold his Majesty face to face, as he is in himself" (Cf. Treatise on the Love of God).

We see by this explanation how the Divine Essence is by grace given to us, as intimately united to our soul as the sacred Body of our Lord is united to our body in the Holy Eucharist. It is in the most perfect sense the "supersubstantial Bread" for which our Savior bids us ask. It is a food, because it makes us strong and great, and a drink, because it inebriates us with God's delights. How great, O God, must be that dignity which you have granted us by the divine grace of sonship, by which we deserve to obtain such a Bread! Give us the grace that, conscious of our high dignity, we may neither ask nor desire any Bread but the Divine one which is yourself, by which you nourish us unto eternal life. "Grant, O Lord," let us say with St. Bonaventure, "that we may always hunger after you, the food of Angels, the refreshment of holy souls, our daily supersubstantial food, which possesses all sweetness, grace, and deliciousness. Let my heart always hunger after you, whom the Angels desire to behold. Let my innermost soul enjoy it and be filled with its heavenly sweetness. Let it continually thirst for you, O Fountain of eternal light, Torrent of delight, and Abundance of the house of God!"

6. LIBERTY AND EQUALITY BESTOWED UPON MERE MORTALS BY DIVINE GRACE

What could be more beautiful and consoling than those words of our Lord: "I no longer speak of you as slaves. . . . Instead, I call you friends" (John 15:15).

Well might St. Gregory the Great exclaim: "Oh, how great is the mercy of our Creator! we are not his worthy servants and he calls us now his friends." Two things are required for perfect friendship—liberty and equality—and both are given to us by divine grace. The Apostle tells us, "Where the Spirit of the Lord is, there is liberty," and divine grace raises the immortal soul to a great degree of union with God, and even to a likeness with him, so that the distance between him and God is no longer so great as to make him utterly unworthy of his friendship. How exquisitely is the value of a friend described in Holy Writ! "A faithful friend is a sturdy shelter, he who finds one finds a treasure. A faithful friend is beyond price, no sum can balance his worth. A faithful friend is a life-saving remedy" (Ecclus. 6:14-16). And where shall we find fidelity such as we find it in him, who, having been made man and died for us on the Cross, now gives himself to us and abides with us forevermore under the form of bread and wine? Should we not say to our hearts: Without a friend you cannot well live, and if Jesus be not your Friend above all, you will be exceedingly sad and desolate. . . . Love him and keep him for your Friend, who when all go will not leave you, nor suffer you to perish in the end" (Following of Christ, bk. II, c. 13).

Some have said: God, having made all things for his own sake, does he not love even his friends for this object alone? True, because it is thus only he could love us, because we, being finite, could not be the object of infinite love. God loves us on account of his infinite goodness, which finds a wonderful reflex in us by divine grace. He loves himself in us and therefore us in himself. He loves us on account of his own divine nature which he has communicated to us by divine grace, and therefore his love for us is most intimate and divine.

God is our friend only in order to benefit and enrich us, and as he has set no bounds to his liberality toward us, so we should make him a return by unbounded love and devotion. "What is man, that you make much of him, or pay him any heed" (Job 7-17). "Doubtless," says St. Bernard, commenting on these words, "man is as vanity, and as nothing, but should he be absolutely nothing who is thus glorified by God? Courage, my brethren! Though we be nothing in our hearts, the heart of God may perhaps contain something of us! O Father of mercy! O God of the wretched; why do you set your heart upon us? Since you have said, 'Where your treasure is, there also is your heart,' must we not then be your treasure if your heart is with us? How, then, can we be a mere nothing if we are your treasure?"

The mystic writer Richard of St. Victor tells us that there are four degrees of love. To the first he gives the name of the insuperable love, because it can be displaced by no other. To the second the name of the inseparable love, because it is so firmly impressed on the memory that it cannot be effaced. To the third he gives that of the exclusive love, because it will endure no rival, and the fourth he calls the insatiable love, because it can never be satisfied.

That man should be irresistibly drawn toward God, as to the highest Good and Beauty, and the Source of all love and happiness, should surprise no one. But that God should be attracted to man can only be accounted for by the fact that in implanting divine grace in his immortal soul God has given him a supernatural beauty which reflects his own nature and divinity and makes him worthy of his love. It was the love of man, a truly insuperable one, which caused him to descend from the highest heavens to the bosom of the humble Virgin, so that, as St. Basil says, He who subdues all is himself vanquished by love of man. Therefore, the divine Spouse of the Song of Songs calls his beloved, the soul adorned with grace, "terrible," and compares her to "an army set in battle array," and says that she has wounded him with one of her eyes. And this love of our God for us is likewise one that inseparably attaches him to us, for has he not told us: "Can a mother forget her infant, be without tenderness for the child of her womb? Even should she forget, I will never forget you" (Isaiah 49:15). As long as we are in a state of grace, so long will God abide in us and with us, because "His delight is to be with the children of men." God loves us all with an absolutely exclusive love, as if each one of us was the only object of it. Thus, in the Song of Songs he calls all his friends: "my beloved, my beautiful one" (Song of Songs 2:10). For though there are many, yet they all shine with the same light of divine grace, all partake of the same divine nature and all enjoy the same love whole and entire, since this love is capable of embracing one as well as many, and many as well as one. Finally, the love of God for an immortal in a state of grace is truly an insatiable one. He would fain take entire possession of it. He says of himself that he is a jealous God. He spoke to all the immortal souls of men from the Cross when he said: "I thirst." For even then he had not satisfied his love for us. Had it been necessary, he would gladly have suffered yet more for our salvation.

7. BEAUTY OF IMMORTAL SOUL IS EMBELLISHED BY DIVINE GRACE

Beauty is the principal object of pure love. If, then, God embraces our immortal soul with such ineffable love, we may conclude from this that our soul must have received a great and heavenly beauty from divine grace, because divine love not only estimates things at their true value, but it is also powerful enough to make the object worthy of being so loved. Human love presupposes love in its object, divine love, on the other hand, works in the immortal soul and produces it. Just as human nature possesses nothing but what it receives from God, he can love the soul only, inasmuch as he makes it partake of his infinite goodness and beauty. This is true of all love of God and of the beauty and goodness of created things, but it applies specially to the supernatural beauty of spiritual creatures. Since, therefore, the love of God works in us by divine grace, and rests upon us on account of it, it must be divine grace that contains this beauty and confers it upon us. Divine grace impresses upon the soul, as on a mirror, a perfect image of the divine nature, so that he who would represent to himself the beauty of an immortal soul in a state of grace ought first to have beheld God himself in his divine perfections. "To a soul in a state of grace," says St. Ambrose, "God speaks as he did once to his chosen city: 'Behold, Jerusalem, I have painted your walls in a splendour of light' " (Hex., lib. VI., cap. 7). Blosius, the great mystic of the sixteenth century, says that it is certain that if we could behold the beauty of an immortal adorned with divine grace, we should be enraptured with delight and wonder. God having revealed this sight to St. Catherine of

Siena, she covered with kisses the footsteps of those who were engaged in bringing sinners back to repentance. Transported by joy, she said to her confessor: "Had you, my father, beheld the beauty of an immortal soul adorned with divine grace, you would certainly for the sake of one such soul gladly suffer death a thousand times."

The ineffable love which God bears to an immortal soul in the state of grace, and the supernatural beauty with which he invests it, lead to that blessed union of which St. Paul speaks in his Epistle to the Ephesians, "Matrimony," he explains, "is a great sacrament"—that is, a mystery of sublime significance, because it typifies the union of Christ with his Church, and therefore also of God with the soul. But the union between husband and wife, however sacred and intimate, is but a shadow of the infinitely closer union of which it is a symbol. For, as the Apostle says: "He who adheres to a wife is made one body, but he who adheres to the Lord is one spirit" (Eph. 5:29-33). And as the spirit, much more the Spirit of God, is exalted above the flesh, so is the union of God exalted above that of man and wife. This union of the soul with God is so true and intimate that its equal cannot be found in all created nature and no reason can comprehend it. God immerses the immortal soul in an ocean of his divine light, inundates it with a stream of divine happiness, fills it with the whole plenitude of his Being and embraces it so closely that no power in heaven or earth can separate it from him. To have God for our Father, our brother, and our friend, would be sufficient to prove the love he entertains for the immotal soul in a state of grace. However, as he would set no bounds to his love of the children of men, he also calls himself their Spouse. This union removes all barriers that might separate the soul from God. As his child she was restrained by filial reverence, as his friend she could not yet claim him, but as Spouse she approaches him without embarrassment, possesses him of right and may exclaim like the Spouse in the Song of Songs, "My Beloved to me, and I to him, who feeds among the lilies." "I to my Beloved, and his turning is toward me." How great should be the desire of the devout soul to please him who has manifested such astounding love for her! Should she not endeavor to love and serve him alone, and exhibit herself according to his desire, "without stain or wrinkle or anything of that sort" (Eph. 5:27), holy and without blemish?

St. Thomas says the three gifts of matrimony which constitute its honor and happiness are (1) fidelity, (2) sanctification, (3) fecundity. Fidelity indicates the indivisible unity of marriage by which husband and wife belong exclusively to each other. The sanctification, or sacrament, indicates the indissolubility of the tie, which, made by God, can never be put asunder. Children, finally, are the special blessing conferred by God on the marriage state.

What fidelity could equal that of our good God? "Husbands, love your wives," the Apostle says, "as Christ loved the Church. He gave himself up for her" (Eph. 5:25). God gives himself to his spouse whole and undivided. If he has elected countless spouses besides each one of us, none the less does he belong entirely to us, nor is his love lessened on that account. He is as the sun which sheds its rays on a thousand eyes, and yet is enjoyed in its entirety by each single one. Rejoice, rather, at the greatness and power of your Beloved, and in the happiness of these countless souls which share his love with you and yet take nothing from it.

The bond of union between God and the faithful soul is as inviolable as the word of God. And has he not said, "I have loved you with an everlasting love," and again, "I will betroth you in faith"?

Fecundity, the third blessing attached to holy matrimony, likewise attends this blessed union of God with the immortal soul, and it may even be said to attain therein to its highest perfection. As the dew falling from heaven fructifies the plant, so does divine grace fructify the soul. Likewise, as the sun by its light enters the eye and is reflected on it, so does the Son of God produce in the immortal soul the image of his Divine Being, and is, as it were, born again in the immortal soul. A heathen philosopher wisely remarks that the offspring of virtue is, or should be, preferred to the posterity of the body. Where have such marvels of holy fecundity been seen as we read of in the lives of the Saints and Servants of God? And should not all souls closely united to their divine Spouse produce, by his merciful assistance, abundant fruit of holy desires and good works to manifest their gratitude and their love, and thus to become ever more united to him?

8. OUR INCORPORATION WITH JESUS BY DIVINE GRACE

We have hitherto sought to explain the mystery of the union of the immortal soul with God by divine grace by comparing it to human relationships. But there is one point in which it transcends all these: and that is that the effect of divine grace is to cause us, in a very deep and true sense, to grow into one being, one body and one spirit with him. God in his infinite unity and perfection can unite himself to Angels and men in the same way as the immortal soul is united to the body which is vivified by it. The creature, without ceasing from being distinct from God, is made one with him in the same manner as in man soul and body, the head and members are one. It is of this sublime unity that Christ spoke after the Last Supper, when he prayed to his heavenly Father: "I have given them the glory you gave me that they may be one, as we are one—I living in them, you living in me—that their unity may be complete" (Iohn 17:22-23). And again he said: "I do not pray for them alone. I pray also for those who will believe in me through their word, that all may be one as you, Father, are in me, and I in you; I pray that they may be (one) in us, that the world may believe that you sent me" (John 17:20-21).

St. Cyril of Alexandria teaches that after the image of the unity which exists in the Blessed Trinity we are to enjoy a twofold, true, and real unity with God, of which the one represents and brings with it the other —namely, the unity of the spirit with the Son of God in his divine nature, and the unity of body with him in his human nature. In his human nature the Son of God unites us in truth, and not only in love, or by the imagination, but in reality, in one Mystical Body of which he is the Head. In the same manner he will make our immortal soul one spirit with his divinity.

St. Chrysostom has the following beautiful thoughts on our union with the sacred humanity of Christ. " 'The body is one and has many members, but all the members, many though they are, are one body; and so it is with Christ,' says the Apostle (I Cor.

12:12). Why do I speak of a participation of union? *We are ourselves the body of Christ.* For what is the bread upon the altar? The body of Christ. And what do they become that receive it? The body of Christ—not many bodies, but one body. As the bread is a whole composed of many grains, and the separate grains nowhere appear, and in their union do not show the distinction though they continue to exist, so we are united among ourselves and with Christ. You are not nourished by one body, and another one by another body, but all by the same body. And therefore the Apostle says: 'Because the loaf of bread is one, we, many though we are, are one body, for we all partake of the one loaf' " (Cor. 10:17).

Again, our Savior has said: "The man who feeds on my flesh and drinks my blood remains in me, and I in him" (John 6:57). St. Cyril, commenting on these words, says: "It is of importance to notice that Christ will be in us, as he himself says, not merely by a certain relation of love, but by a real union. For as two pieces of wax placed and molten together are made one whole, so are we united to Christ by the reception of his body and blood."

The natural bread is also united with the body of him that partakes of it. But since it is a dead and perishable bread, it cannot convert the bodies of the partakers into its own substance. The Body of Christ, however, is a living, undivided, imperishable Bread, and therefore it unites with itself the bodies of those that receive it, makes them its members, and fills them with the plenitude of divine life. Our Lord said: "I am the vine, you are the branches" (John 15:5). Thus the vine feeds with its sap the branches united with it, and penetrates and vivifies them with its own vitality.

Now, the union of our body with the Body of Christ is only the means and figure of that union which divine grace establishes between our immortal soul and the Divinity. We are made one spirit with God as truly and really as the Body of which Christ is the Head must be vivified by the same Spirit in whom the Son of God lives. Accordingly, St. Paul says: "Make every effort to preserve the unity which has the Spirit as its origin and peace as its binding force. There is but one body and one Spirit, just as there is but one hope given all of you by your call. There is one Lord, one faith, one baptism; one God and Father of all, who is over all, and works through all, and is in all" (Eph. 4:3:6). We are, then, truly made one spirit with God, not as if the substance of our soul ceased to exist, but because it is so intimately united with God, as if, in a certain sense, it formed one whole. In the human body, too, the members are substantially distinct from the head, and the soul from the body. Yet they are really one, because they form a whole and cannot exist apart. So are we made one with God, because as Christ has said, we abide in him and he in us.

This doctrine throws still more light upon what has been said previously about the deification of the soul. There it was said that our immortal soul was deified by a supernatural likeness to God, the mystical union with God which is inseparable from it completes this likeness.

We distinguish in the Sacred Humanity of Christ a twofold deification: the one consists in its personal union with the Eternal Word, the other, in its glorification by the communication of divine grace. True, we are not united to one person with God as is the humanity of Christ—nevertheless, our union is so intimate that supernaturally we exist in God and for God, so that this union can find its model only in the union that exists between the divinity and humanity in Christ.

Thus that great mystery is prepared and begun in us which, according to the words of the Apostle, will form the highest perfection of created nature—that God will be All in all. God will be in us not only because he has created us, not only because our whole nature and being is dependent on him, not only because we are his as the work of his hands and reveal his glory, but because he has drawn us entirely unto himself and poured himself out in us; because he absorbs us and unites us to himself as a drop of water is absorbed in a flagon of wine, and because he bears us in his bosom as he does his only begotten Son with whom he is perfectly One.

Let us not fear to lose ourselves in this ineffable union with God. We are lost in an unfathomable abyss, but an abyss not of annihilation, but of the greatest glory and happiness. We lose ourselves to find ourselves again in God, or, rather, to find God himself with all his glory and beatitude. For the more we are God's, the more he is ours. The more we live in him and for him, the more he lives in us and for us. Hence, by the very fact that we are deified in a twofold manner, we also partake in a twofold manner of the divine beatitude: first by beholding the beauty and bliss of God as he himself beholds and enjoys it, and again by possessing this glory and bliss by divine grace—calling it our own as God possesses it and calls it his own in virtue of his nature.

Can human reason comprehend, or the human heart bear the transport with which it learns, that its members are members of Christ, and that its spirit is so closely united with the divine Spirit? Where may we find a thousand tongues and hearts to praise and love so merciful a Father!

Oh that our heart could die to itself and become absorbed in the divine heart of our loving Savior, so that, a heavenly life having begun in it, it should no longer feel its own impulses, but those of God! Then would happen to us in a mystical manner what has happened to some of the Saints of God, whose heart he took from their breast and put his own in its place.

Another sublime advantage which we derive from this union with God by divine grace is that we are made one body and one spirit, not only with the Blessed Trinity, but with the souls of the just. The same Holy Spirit, who, according to St. Augustine, is the bond of union between the Father and the Son likewise embraces us all and unites us as intimately with each other as the soul unites the different members of the body. As a golden chain he links us to God and Christ, and likewise with the choirs of blessed spirits, with the band of Apostles and countless number of holy Martyrs, Confessors, and Servants of God. By this unity the joy we shall experience in the beatific vision in heaven will be multiplied and infinitely increased, as St. Anselm proclaims in moving words: "Human heart, poor heart that suffers so many tribulations—yes, is inundated with suffering—how you would rejoice if you possessed all things that are prepared for you in heaven! Ask your inmost self whether it could comprehend such happiness. Yet, certainly, if another whom you love as yourself possessed the same happiness as you, your joy would be doubled, as you would rejoice no less at his happiness than at your own. But if two or three or many more enjoyed the same good fortune, you would rejoice for each individually as for yourself, if you loved each of them as yourself. In that perfect love, then, of numberless Angels and Saints, where one loves another no less than himself, everyone will rejoice for all others individually as much as for himself. If the heart of man cannot comprehend the joy of so great a good, how will it be wide enough for so many and such great joys? And, indeed, since each rejoices as much at the fortune of another as he loves him, they all, loving God in that perfect happiness incomparably more than themselves and all others, will also rejoice more at the happiness of God than at their own, and that of all others. . . . My Lord and my God, my Hope and the Joy of my heart! Tell my immortal soul whether this is the joy of which you said through your Son: 'Ask, and you shall receive that your joy may be full.' For I have found a joy that is full and more than full" (Prosl., cap. 25, 26).

III

On the Effects and Fruits of Divine Grace

On the Effects and Fruits of
Divine Grace

1. DIVINE GRACE BESTOWS THE LIGHT AND FLAME OF THE HOLY SPIRIT

The Fathers and Doctors of the Church have sometimes called divine grace the light of God—the sublime image of God being for the spiritual world what the sun is for the material world. The Apostles also constantly use light as a symbol of wisdom and knowledge. "God is light," St. John says, "and in him there is no darkness" (John 1:5), and St. James speaks of "Every worthwhile gift, every genuine benefit . . ." descending from the "Father of heavenly luminaries" (James 1:17). Divine grace, as the best and most perfect gift, is also the purest and most sublime light. It is that light by which we are introduced into the inaccessible light of God, which reveals to us the glory of God in all its depths and lets us behold it unveiled and face to face.

By divine grace we are born of the light of God and the fire of the Holy Spirit. We are made "children of light" and children of God. As St. Paul says: "There was a time when you were darkness, but now you are light in the Lord" (Eph. 5:8). Therefore St. Peter, addressing souls in a state of grace, tells them: "You, however, are a chosen race, . . . to proclaim the glorious works of the One who called you from darkness into his marvelous light" (I Peter 2:9). So strikingly true is the figure of light that we can scarcely speak of divine grace without calling it the light of grace. And the Roman Catechism, in explaining divine grace, says: "It is, as it were, a brilliant light that effaces all those stains which obscure the lustre of the soul, and invests it with increased brightness and beauty" (De Caput, II, 59). The Fathers constantly use the expression of the Sacrament of Illumination for Baptism, by which we are regenerated by divine grace. The parallel between the sun's rays and the light of divine grace may be drawn out at great length. For as light penetrates and transforms and vivifies material bodies with which it comes in contact, so does grace penetrate the soul, and transforms it with divine beauty and splendor. As light illumines the eye, enabling it to see objects which otherwise would be invisible to it, so does grace light up the eye of the soul, or rather, grants it a new organ of vision by which it may behold a new world. By reason we only perceive the exterior side of truth—that is, the reflex of truth, in the created world, but not the eternal truth itself in its innermost nature. By the light of divine grace we are enabled to perceive *here* by faith, *hereafter* by vision, that life invisible whence the visible world was produced. It introduces us even into the bosom of God, and lets us look into the mysterious depths which only the Eternal Father and his only begotten Son, and the Holy Spirit, can in virtue of their nature behold. St. Paul says: "For God, who said, 'Let light shine out of darkness,' has shone in our hearts, that we in turn might make known the glory of God shining on the face of Christ" (II Cor. 4:6). Light gives out heat, and when in appearance it is without heat it is only on account of imperfect communication. In the divine Sun, like the material one, light and heat are inseparably united. From the light of the Father and Son proceeds the divine flame of love, the Holy Spirit. The action of God in our hearts kindles not only the light of faith, but also that of his divine love.

The light of the sun calls forth life which had been dormant, and preserves and invigorates it. Divine grace has the same effect on the soul. As a mirror on which the sunlight has been thrown reproduces perfectly the features which are reflected in it, so through divine grace the true and living image of God is reproduced in our minds and hearts, and this imaging of God will be vivid in proportion to their holiness and purity. The less we defile our soul with venial sin, or stain it with too great attachment to creatures, the more will the light of divine grace dwell in us and illumine our soul. "Blest are the single-hearted for they shall see God" (Matt. 5:8).

2. DIVINE GRACE DESTROYS THE DARKNESS OF MORTAL SIN

The first effect of the light of grace, when it is infused in regeneration, is to destroy the darkness of mortal sin. Sin, besides being the object of the hatred of the all-holy God, is the cause of all the evils and misfortunes that befall the world or have befallen it since the fall of our first parents. Famine, plagues, all the wars which have devastated the world and have been the cause of untold suffering to the human race, are the consequence and punishment of sin. The only cure for this evil is the precious blood of the Son of God, which, being shed for us on Mount Calvary, has reconciled sinners with the Father. We have but to imbibe the stream of divine grace which flows from the side of Christ for the cleansing of our sins to be nourished and vivified anew. By divine grace we are changed from enemies into children of God. We may appear before him with confidence, to appease his anger, for we have put on Christ and his justice, and thus are perfectly pleasing to the heavenly Father. As little as God can hate his only begotten Son, so little can he hate those who by grace are made his living members, and bear his image in them. In healing our immortal soul, divine grace does not leave the smallest trace of mortal sin behind. It does not always destroy the inclination to sin which is the fruit of evil habits, but it removes all its guilt. Thus, as St. Paul says: "There is no condemnation now for those who are in Christ Jesus" (Rom. 8:1). If our "sins are as scarlet," God assures us by his prophet, "they shall be made as white as snow, and if they were as red as crimson they shall be white as wool." Scarcely had David confessed to the Lord that he had sinned, when he heard that his sin was taken away. No sooner had he said that he would confess against himself his injustice, than his wickedness was immediately forgiven. He was reconciled to God, and from a slave of Satan he was converted into a great servant of God.

3. DIVINE GRACE INFUSES THE VIRTUES OF FAITH, HOPE AND CHARITY

Divine grace, according to the teaching of the Council of Trent, having eradicated sin from the soul of man, works his sanctification, and infuses into him the three theological virtues of faith, hope and charity.

The natural life of the soul, which distinguishes it from animals, consists in the natural acts of the reason and the will. The supernatural life is that activity which proceeds from the same faculties of intellect and will, but only after these faculties are glorified by divine grace, and converted into new heavenly faculties. In the same way that grace transforms the nature of the soul, and makes it partaker of the divine nature, so it glorifies also its faculties and causes them to be capable of performing acts of a dignity proper only to the divine nature. And to this supernatural ability, which can be implanted only by grace, theologians give the name of infused virtue.

Infused virtue is, then, very different from the so-called acquired virtues. These consist in a certain readiness acquired by our efforts, and by practice, whereby we perform acts *naturally* possible with greater decision and ease. These virtues may be compared to that fruitfulness which careful irrigation and pruning gives to trees, which causes them to produce in greater abundance. Whereas, the infused virtues are similar to a tree upon which a plant of infinitely superior merit has been grafted, and which in consequence grows a fruit which the original stock was incapable of producing. These three virtues of faith, hope and charity have also been called divine virtues, because they unite us in a divine manner with God, have him for their immediate motive and can be produced in us only by a communication of the Divine Nature. God therefore endows his children with these virtues, so that they may even while on earth, in a land of exile, lead a life worthy of their exalted regeneration and be united to him who for all eternity will be the Cause of their beatitude. For the life that the children of God already lead on earth must be of the same kind as the life that awaits them in heaven. In heaven they shall know God as he knows himself, and possess and enjoy him as he possesses and enjoys himself. But as, according to the teaching of the Church, it is necessary for such knowledge and possession of God that the light of glory should transform the faculties of our immortal soul and deify them, so must the faculties of our immortal soul be transformed in this life, so as to be able to know, and love, and confide in God here, in order to attain to eternal happiness with him in heaven. God, who has made us his children and the heirs of his heaven, gives to every creature all that is necessary for the attainment of its end. By divine grace, therefore, he endows his children with those virtues without which they cannot be united with him in a supernatural manner. The Christian is cast upon the stormy sea of life to seek the port of heaven. God in these divine virtues gives faith as a compass to guide his boat aright, hope as a sure anchor, and love as the mighty propelling power which will bear him swiftly to the haven of eternal rest.

4. DIVINE GRACE BESTOWS SUPERNATURAL LIGHT AND STRENGTH

If by grace we partake of the nature of God, we

must also partake of the knowledge proper to the divine nature. We must, as the Apostle says, know God in the same manner as we are known. Only when divine grace is perfected in us in the light of glory will this take place in a perfect manner. But even in the land of exile God will not forsake his children. Even here they shall know him, and their own dignity and the greatness of their inheritance. And as no one knows the Father but himself, and his Son with the Holy Spirit, he must reveal himself by his own Word. Since we cannot by nature grasp or comprehend this divine Word, he has endowed us with a supernatural light and strength whereby we may attain to this knowledge. Our Blessed Savior says, "No one can come to him except the Father draw him" by that supernatural attraction which transcends all earthly experience. The act of faith is an absolutely supernatural one, exceeding all the powers of man. Divine grace bestows on us a super-natural light and a supernatural strength, both of which are necessary for divine faith. In order to be-lieve, it is necessary to know that it is God himself who speaks to us. This we may know by our natural reason. But unless God illuminated our mind and purified our heart we should be incapable of grasping divine truth or making any act worthy of salvation. For the truths of religion are of so sublime a nature that the light of reason is as insufficient to understand them as to reveal them to us. A man born blind may receive an accurate account of objects invisible to him, but they must still remain unknown and incom-prehensible to him. Our condition with regard to supernatural truth would be the same if God who reveals them to us by his Word, did not at the same time infuse into us the supernatural light of grace and bring home these truths to us by means of it.

Let us not be afraid, therefore, to submit our reason obediently to faith. Rather, let us glory in this submission, and thank God, with St. Peter, that "He has called us into his admirable light."

That this light is but darkness when compared with the daylight of eternity, who can deny? But it is a darkness similar to the twilight which precedes the dawn. For, as the Apostle tells us, "Faith is the substance of things hoped for, the evidence of things that appear not."

Faith, then, is a night in comparison to the day of eternal glory. But it is a night illumined with heavenly light, and is as the brightest day in contrast with the light of sense and reason. The grace of faith as far surpasses all natural knowledge as the eye that sees is superior to the one that is blind, or the rational soul of man to the irrational brute.

Oh! that we devoted half the trouble and sacrifices which the learned undergo for the attainment of science, to increase in us the light of faith, so that it should be to us what it was to the holy Apostle, who rejoiced that he knew nothing except Jesus Christ, and him crucified.

5. DIVINE GRACE IS THE VERY FOUNDATION OF THE VIRTUE OF HOPE

Hope, like charity, has its seat, not in the intellect, but in the will. The will has two acts: the first is to take pleasure in the good it sees, and the second to pursue it with earnestness and confidence. In the same way as faith communicates to our reason a supernatural power of understanding, the infused virtue of hope endows our will with a divine power and a supernatural confidence, that it may actively pursue and securely attain the highest and infinite good to which nothing created can attain. Hope lifts us above all creatures in order to rest in God alone. It is the source of our confidence of possessing God, the highest supernatural good, for all eternity, and it bases this confidence upon nothing less than the infinite and almighty power of God himself and the promises made to us by him.

St. Paul has been called the Apostle of divine grace. As grace is the foundation of hope, he more than any of the sacred writers has made holy hope the subject of his discourse. In his Epistle to the Romans he goes at length into the grounds we have for hope: "Now that we have been justified by faith, we are at peace with God through our Lord Jesus Christ. Through him we have gained access by faith to the grace in which we now stand, and we boast of our hope for the glory of God. But not only that—we even boast of our afflictions! We know that affliction makes for endurance, and endurance for tested virtue, and tested virtue for hope. And this hope will not leave us disappointed, because the love of God has been poured out in our hearts through the Holy Spirit who has been given to us" (Rom. 5:1-5). Again, in the eighth chapter of the same Epistle he returns to the same subject in these words: "There is no condemnation now for those who are in Christ Jesus. The law of the spirit, the spirit of life in Christ Jesus, has freed you from the law of sin and death. . . . Yes, we know that all creation groans and is in agony even until now. Not only that, but we ourselves, although we have the Spirit as first fruits, groan inwardly while we await the redemption of our bodies.

In hope we were saved. But hope is not hope if its object is seen; how is it possible for one to hope for what he sees? And hoping for what we cannot see means awaiting it with patient endurance" (Rom. 8:1-2; 22-25). And again in another place: "Praise be to God, who has given us the victory through our Lord Jesus Christ."

What can we add to these sublime words, except that they are given to us not only to be admired, but to be deeply pondered over, so that with the help of divine grace they may give rise to the spirit of child-like confidence in God, which more than any other dispositions makes our soul pleasing to him. For as a great Saint has said, "The measure of our loving confidence in God is the measure of his mercies to us."

6. SUPERNATURAL CHARITY IS A PRECIOUS GIFT OF GOD

"There are in the end three things that last: faith, hope, and love, and the greatest of these is love" (I Cor. 13:13). It is the greatest because it is the complement and perfection of faith and hope. By charity we embrace the highest good which we know by faith, by charity we are united on earth with that which is the object of our hope in heaven. Faith and hope may be dead—i.e., they may exist in us without uniting us in a living manner to God, whilst charity cannot be dead, because it is life in itself and gives life to faith and hope. We may possess the faith and hope of the children of God, without being in a state of grace. But when charity is infused into our immortal soul, then the Holy Spirit is likewise given us. And he comes not only to enrich us with his divine grace, but to dwell in us and consecrate our immortal soul as his temple.

This supernatural charity therefore is as great a gift as sanctifying grace itself. As God unites himself in a supernatural manner to our immortal soul by divine grace, so we unite ourselves by supernatural love in a mysterious but very real manner with God, and thus complete that golden circle which embraces God and the creature and makes both one spirit. God bestows upon us a love which can only be compared to that which he bears his own Son by making us participate in the divine nature, and we again approach and return to our heavenly Father by filial love, as we have proceeded from him, and the same Holy Spirit which proceeds from the Father and the Son becomes the bond and seal of our union with God.

As grace is a participation of the divine nature, so is the charity which proceeds from divine grace a participation of divine charity. Hence some theologians have erroneously held that it was identical with the Holy Spirit himself. Rather is it, according to the Apostle, infused into our hearts by the Holy Spirit, being a holy flame which his sacred fire kindles in our immortal soul, which is an image of that divine charity from which he himself proceeds, as the immediate beatific vision is a participation of that divine intelligence of which the Eternal Word is born. Only such a love becomes the state of the children of God. In grace he loves us with a paternal love in his only begotten Son, and so we must by grace embrace him with filial love. By divine grace he comes to us with the whole goodness and benignity of his divine nature, and so divine grace must pervade our immortal soul as with a divine magnetism that draws us supernaturally to God and immerses us in him.

Love in general is the cause of all that is sweetest and most blessed in our relations with God or with creatures. Its very name is synonymous with consolation and happiness. Our heart has been created for the enjoyment of love, and it desires nothing more than to find a worthy object of love with which to unite itself. Yet what is all natural love for creatures, and even for God, when compared with that holy supernatural charity which is poured out into our hearts by the Holy Spirit in grace? His love comes directly from God himself. It is the blossom and fruit of divine life and happiness, a spark of the fire of divine charity with which he is inflamed. It is of this love that Thomas a Kempis says: "Nothing is sweeter than love, nothing stronger, nothing higher, nothing wider, nothing more pleasant, nothing fuller or better in heaven or earth. For love proceeds from God, and cannot rest but in God above all things created. Whosoever loves knows the cry of this voice. A loud cry in the ear of God is the ardent affection of the soul which says: 'O my God, my Love! You are all mine, and I am all yours'" ("Following of Christ," bk. III, c. 5).

Of this love St. Bernard writes: "It forgets the reverence and submission proper to a creature, and with the hardihood of a child and the familiarity of a spouse boldly raises itself up to God himself, clasps him as its Father, Friend, Beloved, in a most intimate embrace. It penetrates into the innermost depths of his goodness and is dissolved in the abyss of his Divine Heart" (In Cant., hom. 83).

O human heart, lonely and sad heart that will always love and yet is never satisfied with love! how can you remain closed against this grace of divine love, which alone will satisfy all your cravings, and fill you with the torrent of the pleasure of your God? When your Lord approaches you with such love, how can you refuse to complete that golden circle which will fasten himself to you and you to him! Oh, if you did know the gift of God, like the Samaritan woman you would ask the Savior for the living water, which having tasted, you would never thirst again.

7. HEAVENLY BLENDING OF SUPERNATURAL AND NATURAL VIRTUES AND THE GIFTS OF THE HOLY SPIRIT

As by divine grace we are made true children and friends of God, and God gives all his creatures the power and means to live according to their state and destiny, he must give us, who are his children, the help we require to attain to our supernatural end, which is himself. We must be perfect as our heavenly Father is perfect. Therefore divine grace must not only bestow on us the theological virtues by which we are united to God in faith, hope and charity, but likewise all other virtues which will enable us to live in a manner conformable to our rank as children of God, and to our sublime relation with God and our neighbor. These as distinguished from divine virtues are called *moral* virtues, and they are as superior to the natural virtues, such as are known to the human reason, to infidels and philosophers, as divine grace is superior to nature. With natural moral virtue we may lead good lives as religious, fathers of families or citizens. But by divine grace we walk, not in our own spirit, but in that of the Holy Spirit, who produces in us a heavenly morality, meekness, goodness, temperance, and purity and makes us similar to the Angels, even to God himself. Thus, an act of supernatural virtue differs almost as much from acts which are performed on natural though virtuous motives, as the rational acts of man differ from those of merely sensual and animal life. Moreover, the supernatural virtues have, besides their sublime nature, and in virtue of it, the additional advantage over the natural virtues that they may be acquired in a moment and with comparatively little labor. The natural virtues are the fruit of our efforts, and we often take a long time to acquire them. The supernatural virtues are far above all efforts of ours to acquire. They are the fruit of the Holy Spirit, who infuses them into us, and whose divine grace, as St. Ambrose says, knows no tardiness in action. They enter our heart at the moment when we receive divine grace and charity in justification. The exercise of these virtues, it is true, does not become at once easy and pleasant to us, for our evil habits and inclinations are opposed to them. But they give us light and strength, which, if we correspond with divine grace, will enable us to overcome all obstacles in the practice of them. These supernatural virtues are not all, or even the greatest, of the blessings conferred on us by the indwelling of the Holy Spirit. There are others which are particularly attributed to him, and are called in a special sense gifts of the Holy Spirit.

These gifts are spoken of prophetically by the prophet Isaiah, who applied them to the Sacred Humanity of Christ: "The spirit of the Lord shall rest upon him: a spirit of wisdom and of understanding, a spirit of counsel and of strength, a spirit of knowledge and of fear of the Lord" (Isaiah 11:2). The same Holy Spirit who rested upon the humanity of the Son of God comes to us also when we are in a state of grace, and not in a transient manner, but in order to take possession of our immortal soul, and illuminate it and abide with it forever.

By the acts of the seven virtues which we perform under the impulse and with the help of the seven gifts of the Holy Spirit we acquire likewise the eight beatitudes of which our Lord spoke in the Sermon on the Mount (the conditions for acquiring the beatitudes are seven, according to St. Augustine, because the eighth contains in itself and crowns all the different degrees of justice).

The gift of fear and the virtue of temperance make us truly "poor in spirit" by mortifying our pride and our desire of earthly goods, and thus secure to us the kingdom of God, with its sublime sovereignty and abundant riches.

By the gift of piety and the virtue of justice we practice true meekness, live in peace and harmony with our fellowmen, and thus deserve undisturbed possession of the land of promise.

By the gift of knowledge and the virtue of prudence we acquire holy sorrow, and perceiving the vanity of earthly things and of false reasonings, we seek peace of mind and comfort in God alone. The gift of fortitude and the virtue of holy zeal will create in us a growing hunger and thirst after justice, which will hereafter be satisfied by God with all heavenly blessings.

The gift of counsel, by which the virtue of hope is increased and confirmed, will induce us to practice mercy toward our neighbor, in order that we may find mercy from God.

The gift of understanding and the virtue of faith plunge our heart in the divine light, purify it evermore from sensual attachments, and thus procure for us that purity of heart which makes us worthy of seeing God face to face in heaven.

Finally, the gift of wisdom and the virtue of charity tend to unite us ever more intimately with God and with our neighbor in the enjoyment of the highest good, which implies that peace which makes us true and perfect children of God.

These are not the only means by which the Paraclete, the Comforter, assists man in his passage to eternity. Our Savior, speaking for the last time to his disciples, said of him that: "The Paraclete, the Holy Spirit whom the Father will send in my name, will instruct you in everything, and remind you of all that I told you" (John 14:26). These lessons might be summed up under two headings: (1) love of God; (2) love of man. The twelve fruits of the Holy Spirit of which St. Paul speaks are a token and reminder to God's children of what he taught them when he was on earth. For as he "went about doing good," as it was said of him prophetically, "the bruised reed he shall not break, and the smoking flax he shall not extinguish," as his words were ever merciful and compassionate to the sorrowful, the suffering and the sinner; as he forgave his disciples who denied or deserted him without so much as a word of reproach and besought forgiveness from his heavenly Father for his executioners: so the graces conferred by the Holy Spirit on his faithful followers are a perpetual reminder of what Christ expects from them. "The fruit of the Spirit is love, joy, peace, patient endurance, kindness, generosity, faith, mildness, and chastity" (Gal. 5:22-23).

8. THE NATURE AND SUPREME VALUE OF ACTUAL GRACES

Sanctifying grace brings with it the supernatural helps of the Holy Spirit which go by the name of "actual graces." Even when in a state of divine grace, we require a special attraction and instigation of the Holy Spirit in order to perform a supernatural good work.

The natural faculties of the immortal soul cannot pass into active operation without a stimulus from without, which rouses them from inaction. And since a supernatural power cannot be aroused into action by a natural cause, the Holy Spirit, who has given us the power, must also move it to develop itself, and this influence we call "actual grace." It is necessary for the Holy Spirit to animate these germs of virtue with his breath and inspiration and to diffuse his own light and warmth into them to develop a divine life in them.

Moreover, we must by the acts that we perform in the state of grace rise continually higher, ever ascending to a higher state of grace. But this we are unable to do alone, even with the grace we already possess, because no one can be raised above his condition without the help of a higher agency. The Divine Spirit therefore must prompt us to aspire to a higher degree of divine grace, and assist us to reach it. For this the seven gifts of the Holy Spirit are not sufficient. They indicate a *condition,* and are therefore dormant qualities of our soul till they are brought into activity by him. The gifts of the Holy Spirit make a pliant instrument of our immortal soul, but we need the master hand to play upon it and so bring out its virtue and harmony. Again, every person in the state of justice requires actual grace, not only for the performance of supernatural goods works, but in order to resist temptation to grave sin, and also to avoid the constant temptation to venial sin.

Sanctifying grace makes us children of God. As such we may rightly expect from our heavenly Father the help of his Holy Spirit to develop and foster our supernatural life and guide us in all our ways. By divine grace we are made living members of Christ. And "Chirst," as the Council of Trent tells us, "incessantly imparts his strength to the justified as the head imparts strength to the members and the vine to its branches. And their good works are preceded and accompanied and followed by this strength, and without it they could in no wise be meritorious to God, or acceptable" (Sess. VI, C. 76, de Justif.).

This assistance is a staff placed in our hands, and remains in our possession as long as we ourselves do not cast it away. When we are in a state of divine grace, the Holy Spirit dwells in us as in a temple. He constantly speaks to our heart, teaches us every truth, urges us to the pursuit of all good, warns us against sin, strengthens us in the hour of danger, and supports us when we stumble or are about to fall. Thus are the words of Scripture verified in us: "He found them in a wilderness, a wasteland of howling desert. He shielded them and cared for them, guarding them as the apple of his eye. As an eagle incites its nestlings forth by hovering over its brood, so he spread his wings to receive them and bore them up on his pinions" (Deut. 32:10-11).

9. SANCTIFYING GRACE MAKES US HEIRS OF HEAVEN AS A SURETY OF LOVE FOR ETERNAL REWARD

Divine grace, besides making us true children of God, gives such a value to the works which proceed from it that through these works we may purchase heaven. Thus, God does not grant us heaven gratuitously from pure liberality, nor simply out of fidelity to his promises, but out of strict justice, as a reward due to our works. True, God is not obliged to reward our good works, for as our Creator and Father he might justly claim a right to all our services. Hence heaven is always a reward and a divine grace bestowed upon us—sanctifying grace, which makes us heirs of heaven, and all the faculties by which we perform supernatural works, being the gratuitous gifts of God.

Nevertheless heaven, in the words of St. Paul, is a "grace for grace"—namely, a second grace which the first grace merits for us, and for which it qualifies us. By sanctifying grace we are made partakers of the divine nature, and the works which we perform are divine works. Thus we stand in a relation of equality to heavenly glory, and when God promises us this glory he promises it as an inheritance and a reward which is not above the dignity of our person and the value of our works.

A king is not under an obligation to reward the services that his subjects or children are bound to give him. But his children would have a right to expect a share in his authority and to inherit his riches and his kingdom. It is the same with our heavenly Father. We have not been promised a heavenly reward for the good works which we perform by nature only, for they are in no proportion whatsoever to the dignity of heavenly happiness. Even the supernatural works which we perform when not in a state of grace, by means of actual graces and the virtues of faith and hope, are not worthy of heaven. For we do not yet perform those works as heirs of heaven. And they can only serve to prepare our heart for this filial love, and for the reception of the grace of sonship through the merits of Christ. But when we have actually been made children of God by divine grace, and are united to him by filial love, then all the good works that we perform with the help of divine grace are so many filial services which God can only reward worthily with the riches of his kingdom.

The infinitely precious Blood of the Son of God could alone purchase this grace for us, and the virtue communicated to the works performed by us in and by it is so great as to give them a very high value in the eyes of our heavenly Father. The great and primary distinction between Christ and ourselves is that his merit was due to his natural dignity, and was so abundant that it was sufficient for all Angels and all men, while we have received our dignity through him and can merit heaven only for ourselves.

The children of God are led by his Spirit, as the Apostle says, and their actions become, as it were, the actions of Christ himself. He is the soul and root of their life, and he works through them. "The divine Spirit," writes St. Francis of Sales, "acts in, by, and for us so admirably that, though our actions are our own, they still belong more to him than to ourselves. We perform them in him and by his direction, while he performs them in us. We act for him while he acts for us, and co-operate with him while he co-operates with us" ("Love of God," Bk. II., c. 6). Again, St.

Thomas Aquinas teaches that the value and merit of our actions are to be measured, not by our natural power and dignity, which are but finite, but by the infinite power and dignity of the Holy Spirit who resides in us. (I, 2, qu. 114, a. 3). This is the reason why the Apostle so often calls the Holy Spirit the Spirit of promise, the Pledge of our inheritance, and the Surety of our reward.

Oh incomprehensible dignity, oh inexhaustible wealth of divine grace! When shall we ever be able to appreciate this gift of God, which is the source of all other blessings and gifts? Divine grace it is which causes all our actions, and the sufferings and trials which we meet with in our journey through life, to become so meritorious in the sight of God that it could be said of them: "The present burden of our trial is light enough, and earns for us an eternal weight of glory beyond all comparison" (II Cor. 4:17).

What is it that gives such value to our frequently insignificant and trifling actions but divine grace? Without it we might perform sublime deeds, conquer and convert kingdoms, devote our lives to the service of God and our neighbor, without meriting the smallest share of heavenly glory. With divine grace all that we do is meritorious in his sight. We have but to pronounce the Holy Name with devotion, to offer up our actions and thoughts to God, to give a cup of cold water in his name to a disciple, to suffer the trials and sorrows of life in union with his, and we have merited an eternal reward. In divine grace nothing is small and insignificant. Dipped in grace, the base metal of our actions is changed into pure gold, and is made capable of purchasing heaven and the vision of God for all eternity. Again, let us never forget, we stand higher in the sight of God, for every exercise of this privilege of accumulating merits, in proportion to the love and the frequency with which we perform these acts. Our Lord revealed to St. Catherine of Sienna that the actions performed by human beings were pleasing to him, not in proportion to their greatness, nor to the pain and difficulty with which they were accomplished, but solely by the amount of love we put into them.

With every degree of divine grace we have attained, every Communion we have received, every Mass we have assisted at with devotion, the greater is our dignity in his eyes, and this greater dignity is communicated to our actions, and makes them more pleasing to him. For in his meritorious works the Christian offers up to God not only his actions, but himself.

10. SUFFERINGS AND TRIALS CAN BECOME SUBLIMELY MERITORIOUS FOR HEAVEN IN UNION WITH JESUS AND THE SAINTS

The merit of an increased reward and dignity for all eternity is not the only fruit of the supernatural works which we perform in a state of grace. They have another supreme advantage, which is that they remove the obstacles which may, after death, delay our entrance into heaven. As divine grace makes the good works of the children of God very pleasing to him, and worthy of a heavenly reward, so it makes their sufferings and trials unspeakably meritorious and acceptable to him. We need only suffer with patience and resignation, and God will, in consideration of the high dignity with which we are invested by grace, efface the stains of sin from our immortal soul and remit their temporal punishment. In the same manner as the satisfaction of Christ derives its infinite value from the infinite dignity of his person rather than from the greatness of his sufferings, so the pains and trials of his living members derive a value from divine grace which they would not otherwise possess. Man's ignorance of God, of his holy hatred of sin, of his divine justice, is such that nothing is more common than to hear the purgatorial fires spoken of lightly, almost as if they were of no account. How different this view is from that of the Saints, and of all who have studied the subject in the light of the teaching of the Fathers and Doctors of the Church! We learn from them that, in proportion to the greatness of God's rewards, which exceed all that our imagination can picture to us, is the severity of the punishment he exacts for what are sometimes spoken of as "little sins," which are forgotten, frequently, as soon as they are committed, and so never repented of. The revelations of the Saints point to the same conclusion. More than one speaks of the pains endured in these purifying fires as being greater than any known to man on earth. And their long duration is one of the points on which they have specially insisted. What gratitude, therefore, do we not owe to God for his gift of sanctifying grace, whereby all our actions, and especially the trials and suffering of life endured in a spirit of penance, should acquire such value in his sight as to outweigh our ceaseless offenses against him.

Divine grace causes us also to participate in the merits and satisfactions of the Saints, as well as in those of Christ himself. In the words of the Psalmist we can say: "I am a partaker with all them that fear you and keep your commandments." By divine grace we enter into the most intimate and loving communion with Christ and all the elect, being joined with them into a Mystical Body whose soul is the Holy Spirit. And we profit by their merits and intercession. The merit of the Saints is in itself a personal one, and can only directly increase sanctifying grace for themselves. Nevertheless our fellowship with them in grace is so intimate that their merit also profits us, and effects in us at least indirectly an increase of sanctifying grace.

Another reason we should have for a high esteem for sanctifying grace is its power of breaking down our vicious habits and strengthening our good ones. "Come and behold the works of the Lord, what wonders he has done upon earth," cries the inspired writer. Cassian applies these words to the effects of divine grace. "Come and see," he says, "how a hardened usurer is converted to liberality, a spendthrift and debauchee to continency, a proud man to humility, a self-indulgent and delicate person to severe and zealous penance. These are truly works of God, and miracles which in a moment convert, as in the case of Matthew, publicans into Apostles, and, in that of St. Paul, raving persecutors into most zealous preachers of the Gospel." In the same way St. Augustine testifies to the wonders the grace of God had wrought in his own nature. He had long and laboriously battled with the vanities of this world, with his evil habits and passions. It was only with much difficulty that he could free himself from them. But when divine grace had suddenly burst these chains asunder, he exclaimed: "How sweet on a sudden was it become to me to be without the sweets of those toys! And what I was before so much afraid to lose I now cast from me with joy. For you, O my God, did expel them from me, and did come yourself instead of them, sweeter than any pleasure whatever" (Confess., Bk. IX, C. I).

IV

On Some Prerogatives
of Divine Grace

1. GLORIES AND PRIVILEGES OF DIVINE GRACE ARE INEXHAUSTIBLE

2. DIVINE GRACE ASSURES THE GUIDANCE OF GUARDIAN ANGELS

3. CHRISTLIKE SUPERNATURAL LOVE OF ONE'S NEIGHBOR

4. SIN IS THE PERSISTENT OBSTACLE TO UNION WITH GOD

5. SUBLIME VALUE OF FERVENT PRAYER, THE SACRAMENTS, THE HOLY SACRIFICE OF THE MASS AND DEVOTION TO OUR LADY

On Some Prerogatives
of Divine Grace

1. GLORIES AND PRIVILEGES OF DIVINE GRACE ARE INEXHAUSTIBLE

Notwithstanding all that has been said of divine grace, the list of its glories and privileges is not yet exhausted.

Since divine grace makes us dearly beloved children of God, and he embraces us in ineffable tenderness in his only begotten Son, we may be confident that he will provide for us with paternal solicitude.

"Seek first his kingship over you, his way of holiness, and all these things will be given you besides" (Matt. 6:33), said our Savior. This kingdom of God is no other than divine grace by which God reigns in us and by which we are called to reign with him. If we seek heaven only, earth will likewise be ours. Everything is ours if we belong to Christ and to God.

"All things are yours," writes St. Paul to the Corinthians, "whether it be Paul, or Apollos, or Cephas, or the world, or life, or death, or the present, or the future: all these are yours, and you are Christ's and Christ is God's" (I Cor. 3:21-23). The Saints are ours to assist us, life is ours to make us happy in God, death to bring us to him, the world because it is subject to us and was created for us.

Oh blessed and happy condition! For if we belong to God we are lord over all things. Says St. Bonaventure, "the Lord, the Friend, the Father, will not permit his servant, his friend, his child, to suffer want." God compares his paternal solicitude to that of a mother in order to extol it even more, saying: "Can a mother forget her infant, be without tenderness for the child of her womb? Even should she forget, I will never forget you" (Isaiah 49:15). "Hear me, O house of Jacob, all who remain of the house of Israel, my burden since your birth, whom I have carried from your infancy" (Isaiah 46:3). "Whoever touches you," he likewise says through the prophet Zechariah, "touches the apple of my eye" (Zech. 2:12). And, again, it was said of him: For he will hide me in his abode in the day of trouble; he will conceal me in the shelter of his tent" (Ps. 27:5).

Our Blessed Savior renews these promises in yet more explicit terms. "Do not be concerned," he says, "for your life, what you are to eat, or for your body, what you are to wear. . . . Take the lilies: they do not spin, they do not weave; but I tell you, Solomon in all his splendor was not arrayed like any one of them. If God clothes in such splendor the grass of the field, which grows today and is thrown on the fire tomorrow, how much more will he provide for you, O weak in faith!" (Luke 12:22-28). What should cause us any anxiety if we are in the state of grace? Eternity belongs to us as heirs of heaven, and here on earth God will provide for all our necessities. We may as St. Peter tells us, "Cast all your cares on him because he cares for you" (I Peter 5:7). Though God may not see fit to answer our prayers for temporal blessings and posterity, we can trust him with absolute confidence to know what is best for us. Too often, so weak are we, the things we crave for most ardently in this life would advance us least in the path of salvation and perhaps lead us to eternal ruin. In our own estimation we are wise, but what are we in the sight of God? Truth is often veiled from our eyes. We must estimate it by faith and by the divine Light. "As long as the heir is a child," the Apostle says—that is, as long as he lives in this land of exile—"he differs nothing from a servant, even if he be Lord of all." Though God waits for man to attain his manhood in his eternal home before sharing his heavenly kingdom with him, yet even in this life he gives him a foretaste of the joys that are to come, of the peace that is above all understanding, and the assurance that around him are "the everlasting arms."

2. DIVINE GRACE ASSURES THE GUIDANCE OF GUARDIAN ANGELS

God not only extends his own special and loving protection to those who are in a state of grace, but he gives them his Angels to watch over them. "The Angels of the Lord," Scripture tells us, "shall encamp around those that fear him." That we should give them all honor and reverence seems most fitting. Also that we should look upon ourselves as unworthy of their service. But they know better than we the height to which divine grace has raised our immortal soul, and our dignity as true children and spouses of the King of Glory. They recognize in us the supernatural image of God and the temple of the Holy Spirit. Is it astonishing, therefore, that they willingly help to guard the sacred treasure of divine grace within us? The communication of divine grace and its increase is so great a work that even God can perform no greater work in a pure creature. Thus, as the Apostle teaches, they are "ministering spirits sent to minister to them who shall receive the inheritance of salvation." True, they imitate our heavenly Father in extending their care also to the preservation of our earthly goods, and in protecting us from temporal evils. But this they do because we are by divine grace children of God, and they do so only insofar as our temporal welfare conduces to our heavenly destiny.

The guardianship of the holy Angels, and the example of the Saints, are among the means God has given us to tread the pathway of life securely. The enemy seeks to tempt us, as he did our Divine Savior, with the three idols of riches, pleasure, and power, before which the vast majority of men bow down and adore. The Angel by our side is ever whispering to us that not in such things can true happiness be found. And the Saints by their example show us how to tread those idols underfoot. "You have made us for yourself," exclaims the great St. Augustine, "and our hearts can never rest till they rest in you."

Through grace we possess not only the greatest, but the only happiness which we can enjoy on earth. In grace we take possession of the highest and infinite good not only by hope, but in truth and in reality.

Already in our inmost heart we may embrace it and taste its sweetness. By divine grace we bear God truly and substantially within us. We may call him our own with perfect right and hold him so firmly that no power in heaven or earth can rob us of him. By divine grace we embrace him with the arms of holy charity, press him to our bosom, and are so penetrated by him that we are one heart and one soul with him. By the union with God through divine grace, we experience even in this life at times a joy and sweetness such as no pleasure of the senses ever gave or ever could give, and which are a very foretaste of heaven.

Moreover, divine grace confers upon the immortal soul that sweet and secure peace which the Son of God came on earth to establish in the hearts of men of good will—that peace of Christ of which St. Paul says: "God's own peace, which is beyond all understanding, will stand guard over your hearts and minds, in Christ Jesus" (Phil. 4:7).

As peace is the principal fruit of divine grace, so it is the first condition of happiness. So heavenly is this peace that the world, though it promises many things, does not even undertake to give us peace. And yet without it where is true happiness to be found? And possessed of this great treasure, were we to lose all else, should sorrow and trials of every kind assail us, as long as we possess God we possess all. He alone suffices and where he abides there likewise are true peace and happiness.

3. CHRISTLIKE SUPERNATURAL LOVE OF ONE'S NEIGHBOR

The foundation, the very rock, on which sanctifying grace is built is love of God, that divine fire in the human heart which our Savior said he came on earth to bring. And what would he but that it should be enkindled.

This is the first and greatest commandment, and again he tells us, "the second is like unto the first: You shall love your neighbor as yourself." About the first there can be no mistake. But how many there are who are under a complete delusion about the second! And what is the result? They strive earnestly and genuinely to increase in the love of God knowing that it is the beginning and end of all spiritual life, they lay the altar of sacrifice and prepare the victim, but the divine fire never comes down from heaven to consume it. Their hearts remain cold and dry, and they complain that religion gives them no consolation. In a majority of cases, and especially in that of men and women leading Christian lives who would shrink from the commission of gross sins, and perhaps not be tempted to fall into them, the cause of this lack of heavenly fire is want of supernatural love of their neighbor. The whole of our Divine Savior's life upon earth may be said to have been devoted to this one object: to teach us by word and example the love of our neighbor. The first time he exercised his omnipotent power over his own creation, he did so at our Lady's intercession, in order to save the passing confusion of his host. And he worked it in spite of the fact that his "hour was not yet come." This was but the beginning of that series of acts of gracious mercy, and forgiveness, and healing, which were summed up in the Gospel narrative by the phrase, "He went about doing good." Even more striking are the words of warning he used to his disciples on the same subject: "My command to you is: love your enemies, pray for your persecutors. This will prove that you are sons of your heavenly Father, for his sun rises on the bad and the good, he rains on the just and the unjust. If you love those who love you, what merit is there in that? Do not tax collectors do as much?" (Matt. 5:44-46). "Be compassionate, as your Father is compassionate. Do not judge, and you will not be judged. Do not condemn, and you will not be condemned. Pardon and you shall be pardoned" (Luke 6:36-37). But it was only at the Last Supper, at the crowning moment of his divine earthly career, when the types of the Ancient Law were about to give way before the glorious realities of the New Law, that he unfolded to them the whole length and depth and breadth of this love which was to reign in the hearts of his followers, and which was to be the sign by which all men should know them to be his disciples. He who had said that he came to make all things new put before them a height of self-devotion such as no patriarch or prophet had ever dreamed of, or pagan philosopher so much imagined. "This is my commandment," Jesus said to them, "love one another as I have loved you" (John 15:12).

This, then, is the divine model put before us. And though no mortal can ever hope to attain to it, at least by measuring himself against this example he may realize how far he falls short of it. Above all we should grasp two all-important facts: that the seat of this love, or charity, is in the *heart,* and that it should find expression in the personal service of our neighbor. What could be more inspiring than our beloved Savior's example in this respect? He was not satisfied with healing those who came to him—the lame and the diseased and the blind—at a distance. He chose to come in personal contact with the afflicted, making clay and spreading it on the eyes of the sightless, and taking the hand of the ruler's daughter who was dead and so raising her to life. And, again, we read that mothers "were bringing their little children to him to have him touch them" (Mark 10:13). He entered into the house of Simon the leper, and suffered "the woman who was a sinner" to kiss his feet and moisten them with her tears. The crowd pressed round him, and he rebuked them not. And when his disciples (how like what we should have done!), wearied of the importunity of the woman of Canaan, said, "Send her away, for she cries after us," he only turned to her and praised her faith, and sent her away comforted. But it was not till the eve of his sacred Passion that Christ gave an explanation of his meaning in these words: "After he had washed their feet . . . reclined at table once more. He said to them: 'Do you understand what I just did for you? You address me as "Teacher" and "Lord," and fittingly enough, for that is what I am. But if I washed your feet—I who am Teacher and Lord—then you must wash each other's feet' " (John 13:12-14).

And this personal service must be accompanied with *love*, or, rather, it must owe its source to love and be the very outcome of it. How are we to know that we possess this love, without which we not only cannot claim to be Christ's disciples, but do not even bear an outward resemblance to them? St. Paul, the Apostle and teacher of divine grace, tells us, and in words so precise that there can be no possible mistake about their meaning. In the first place he says that it does not consist in almsgiving—a most illuminating distinction.

"If I give everything I have to feed the poor and hand over my body to be burned, but have not love,

I gain nothing." Then he goes on to explain what it is: "Love is patient; love is kind. Love is not jealous, it does not put on airs, it is not snobbish. Love is never rude, it is not self-seeking, it is not prone to anger; neither does it brood over injuries. There is no limit to love's forbearance, to its trust, its hope, its power to endure" (I Cor. 13:3-5, 7). It is true that Christ said, "Give alms, and all things are clean to you"; but these words were spoken to the Pharisees. Of his own followers he asks more, as he gives more. Nevertheless, almsgiving, especially when given at the cost of personal sacrifice, is immensely pleasing to God, and brings down his choicest blessings on the giver.

The true significance of the "new commandment" which our Savior gave at his Last Supper, and all that he and his holy Apostles have taught about charity, is explained by the doctrine of divine grace. We must love our neighbor because he has been made partaker of the divine nature by grace. By the same means he has been elevated above his own nature. He likewise is unspeakably dear to his Redeemer and is destined, if he persevere to the end, to an eternal weight of glory in heaven.

Not his human nature, but the divine nature which is impressed upon him—not so much he himself, in or by himself, but rather God who is united to him in grace—must be the motive of our love. Therefore we must embrace him with the same supernatural love which we bear toward our good and merciful God himself. Is he not by grace a brother, and, what is more, a living member of Jesus Christ? And can we love Christ without loving at the same time in him, and with him, his brothers and his members? Is he not by grace a temple in which the Holy Spirit resides truly and personally with his whole divinity, as the soul in the body? Can we, then, think of separating in our affection what Divine love has so intimately and inseparably united?

Divine grace, moreover, brings us most closely together in a spiritual manner. We are all children of God, brethren in God, stones of the divine temple, and members of the same Mystical Body of Christ. To each one our Lord's promise is that he will guard them "as the apple of his eye," and that "he that touches you touches me." How, therefore, will he suffer one of his children to be ill-treated, neglected, or maligned, without visiting the culprit with his indignation? "Justice without mercy," it has been said, "to him who judges without mercy." (It was revealed to Ven. Marie de Sales Chappuis that Christ makes excuses, as he did for his executioners, for those who have interpreted their neighbors' actions charitably in life, when they appear before the judgment seat.) So completely does he identify himself with us— with our neighbor as with ourselves—that he promises that he will look upon services rendered to them as if they were done to him. No wonder the beloved disciple, the one who came nearest to learning the secrets of his Sacred Heart, exclaims: "If God so loved us, we also ought to love one another." And St. Paul exhorts us: "Be kind one to another, merciful, forgiving one another, even as God has forgiven you in Christ."

4. SIN IS THE PERSISTENT OBSTACLE TO UNION WITH GOD

The greatest obstacle to our union with God by divine grace is sin. Mortal sin, as we all know, extinguishes divine charity in our soul, and drives us from the arms of God into those of his enemy. But all sin is displeasing to God in the highest degree. To commit even a venial sin is a great misfortune, the greatest that could possibly happen to us in the sight of the all-holy God. Look at the temporal punishments he has inflicted on his servants for sins which we should think little of committing. Moses, for instance, for a slight disobedience to his commands, and David for a vainglorious action in counting the people of Israel. The Saints, with a clearer sight of the unutterable majesty and purity of God, reach a much nearer comprehension of the nature and heinousness of sin. St. Teresa, after commenting on sins due to inadvertency, goes on to say: "But from willfully committing any sin, however small, may God deliver us! I cannot think how we could dare to set ourselves against so great a Sovereign, in however small a matter, though no offence against such majesty can be called small, because we know that he is watching us. Such a fault seems to me thoroughly premeditated. It is as if we said: 'Lord, although this displeases you, yet I shall do it.' . . . Is such a misdeed a little one? To me it seems not a little sin, but a great and very great one."

Venial sins, it is true, do not destroy divine charity. But, as St. Francis of Sales tells us, "charity is sometimes weakened and depressed in the affections, till it seems to be scarcely in exercise at all, and yet it remains entire in the supreme region of the immortal soul. This happens when under the multitude of venial sins, as under the ashes, the fire of holy love remains covered, and its flame smothered though it is not utterly extinguished."

Probably the tongue is the most frequent cause

of sin to all, and what terrible things St. James tells us of the power for evil in that "little member"!

"Every form of life . . . can be tamed, and has been tamed, by mankind; the tongue no man can tame. It is a restless evil, full of deadly poison. We use it to say, 'Praised be the Lord and Father'; then we use it to curse men, though they are made in the likeness of God. . . . If one of you is wise and understanding, let him show this in practice through a humility filled with good sense. Should you instead nurse bitter jealousy and selfish ambition in your hearts, at least refrain from arrogant and false claims against the truth. Wisdom like this does not come from above. It is earthbound, a kind of animal, even devilish, cunning. Where there are jealousy and strife, there also are inconstancy and all kinds of vile behavior. Wisdom from above, by contrast, is first of all innocent. It is also peaceable, lenient, docile, rich in sympathy and the kindly deeds that are its fruits, impartial and sincere. The harvest of justice is sown in peace for those who cultivate peace" (James 3:7-9; 13-18).

To sin is to be human, and we need never expect to be wholly free from all venial sins and imperfections as long as we abide in this mortal life. Two thoughts gathered from the teaching of the Saints may be of use to us to help us to fight against these falls which are such an obstacle to our union with God. One is that if, the moment we are conscious of committing a sin, we turn to God with a profound sense of humility and sorrow for having "grieved" his Divine Spirit, whose temple we are, we gain, as St. Francis of Sales tells us, by our fall: "inasmuch as the profit we make by advancing in humility is a rich reparation for the damage sustained by our frailty."

The second is the use of what an ascetical writer calls "the rudder of the devout life, examination of conscience." To quote again from the author of Philothea, "our examination of conscience must be reduced to a search for our passions." In order to do this, we must two or three times a day give a swift passing glance at *our heart*—what it is preoccupied with, what it is doing, for "where our treasure is, there also is our heart." Is it occupied with self and its interests, or with God and his? Is it resentful, critical, vain, dissipated, betrayed into emotions which if laid bare would fill us with confusion? This swift glance will more than any other exercise show us how we stand before God. If our dominant feeling, the one uppermost in our heart, is one displeasing to God, we should humble ourselves before him and implore his forgiveness. Self-examination is the eye of a devout life. Without it we are ever groping in the dark, and shall never reach our goal, which is the union of our soul with God.

5. SUBLIME VALUE OF FERVENT PRAYER, THE SACRAMENTS, THE HOLY SACRIFICE OF THE MASS AND DEVOTION TO OUR LADY

The three principal means by which we advance in the grace of God are prayer, the sacraments, and the Eucharistic celebration. Prayer, though it may be divided into vocal and mental, is in its essence one thing only—that is, the conversation of the immortal soul with God. Cor ad cor loquitur. Mary Magdalen seated at our Lord's feet, listening to the words which fall from his Divine lips, is the example of prayer to all time. True, we may converse with God in words put into our lips by Christ—as in the Our Father—or by the Church, or by the Saints. But in such prayers, unless we put our soul into them, uttering the words with attention and devotion, and thus, as it were, making them our own, they will be but a "vain repetition," against which our Lord so emphatically warned his disciples.

A well-known ascetical writer has said that unless we practice mental prayer our vocal prayer will remain little more than words. Hence, he goes on to say, "the importance of the hour or half-hour we give to meditation. It is the hour in which the soul lives its true life. . . . It is the hour of its intensest discipline, when acts are produced which vibrate long afterwards through the hours of the day, through the spaces of life. It is the hour of speaking to God in his Holy of Holies, where the immortal soul finds insight and strength and endurance. It is the hour of calm, when the thronging elements of one's personal life are ranged in order, and marshalled to obedience, so that the will may aim at one thing, and one thing alone. It is the hour of kindling of that precious fire— the fire of Divine love which must burn through every pulsation of life, or life's deeds can never be borne to the heavens, but must drop like leaves to wither on the earth. It is the hour . . . when the heart speaks to God, and what is of infinitely greater moment, when God speaks to the heart" (A Retreat by Bishop Hedley, p. 244).

Again, there is ejaculatory prayer, of which it has been said that it supplies the place of almost every other kind of prayer, and nothing takes its place. It was by means of ejaculatory prayer that the solitaries of the desert not only attained to sanctity, but reached great heights of contemplation.

Prayer, though it should in the first place be

directed to our wants, to be pleasing to God, must not end there. Our Divine Savior in a revelation to St. Gertrude told her how earnestly he desired that we should make intercession for all men. "Self-love," he said, "has infected the whole world as if it had drunk poison. Do you therefore, my servants, prepare yourselves with supplications, mercy, and anxious desires, grieving over the offensives committed against me, and over the damnation of sinners, and so you will mitigate the wrath of my Divine judgments." We learn from Lancisius that the offering of the Precious Blood of Christ and of his Passion and Death to the Eternal Father, in order to appease him for the sins of the world, is of boundless efficacy.

Intercession for the souls in purgatory, either by indulgenced prayers or practices of piety, is, we know, specially pleasing to God, and will bring down his choicest blessings on our immortal souls. In praying for them we are exercising all the spiritual and corporal acts of mercy, and procuring their powerful advocacy here and hereafter before the throne of God.

It is, however, in the Sacraments, and above all in the Sacrament of the Holy Eucharist, that God has chosen to reserve the full plenitude of his divine graces and mercies to man. We receive him there who is the Author of all good. And he comes, as the Saints tell us, with his arms full of blessings, ready to bestow them on all who have made their hearts empty by humility and large by detachment from creatures. We need not fear to approach him, for, as he himself has said, they that are whole need not the physician, but they that are sick. The best beggars are those who are most sorely in need. We have but to own our necessities and show him our wounds for him to heal us and send us away comforted. To keep away from him would be a false humility, for "to fly him is to fly Life" ("Following of Christ," Bk. IV, C. 6).

But if in the Sacrament of the Altar God does everything for us, as great, or even (if possible) greater, then that is what he enables us to do for him in the Sacrifice of the Mass. In the Mass—astounding privilege!—we make God an offering worthy of himself: the spotless Lamb, who was slain before the beginning of the world. The feelings of Mary, when at the presentation of the Child Jesus in the Temple she presented the Son of God to his Eternal Father—the first of all created beings to make him an offering worthy of himself—should be, as far as our weakness and misery permit, ours also. By faith we see him again born on the altar, as he was born in the stable of Bethlehem. By faith we behold him lifted up by his minister, as he was lifted up long ages ago on the tree of the Cross for the healing of nations. He is there truly present as High Priest and Victim, who is a Priest forever of the Order of Melchisedech: the Advocate with the Father, Jesus Christ the just. The Mass should be the central act of our day, as the Passion is the central act of the world's history. In the Canon of the Mass the priest says: *per ipsum,* through him; *cum ipso,* with him; *in ipso,* in him. Through him come all grace and holiness, perseverance comes from walking with him—in him is life everlasting.

If we wish to make great progress in the spiritual life, we must cultivate a tender devotion to Mary. There is nothing that makes us more pleasing to the Sacred Heart of Jesus than a love of his Blessed Mother. The Saints are unanimous on this point. St. Bernard tells us that she is the channel by which God conveys his blessings on man, and in a well-known passage of his writings he recommends us to make all our offerings through her. For he says our hands may not be free from guilt, but Mary's "are as the whitest lilies, so the Lover of lilies will never be found to reprove what is found in her hands."

Blessed Grignon de Montfort teaches us that the Holy Spirit, the Spouse of the most pure Virgin, willingly dwells in hearts devoted to her, bringing with him his most glorious gifts and fruits, and taking up his abode in them forever. We learn from the same and similar sources that Mary earned her astounding privileges by her humility, and in this we should take her in a special manner as our model and heavenly Mother.

(For an excellent book on OUR LADY, please be kind enough to consult: Bernadot-Doheny: "OUR LADY IN OUR LIFE," Ave Maria Press, 1976, Notre Dame, Indiana 46556.)

V.

Our Lady Introduces Us to the Life of Divine Grace

1. **OUR LADY AND OUR PREDESTINATION**
2. **OUR LADY HAS MERITED GRACE FOR US**
   a. THE ANNUNCIATION
   b. THE PRESENTATION
   c. CALVARY
3. **OUR LADY IS OUR MOTHER**
4. **OUR LADY IS MOTHER OF THE CHURCH**
5. **THE IMMACULATE HEART OF MARY**

Our Lady Introduces Us to the Life of Divine Grace

1. OUR LADY AND OUR PREDESTINATION

"Praised be the God and Father of Our Lord Jesus Christ, . . . God chose us in him before the world began, to be holy and blameless in his sight, to be full of love . . ." (Eph. 1:3,4).

So, from all eternity, God thought of us. He loved us. He chose and called us.

But to what does He call us? To be His children. In His love, He predestinated us unto the adoption of children through Jesus Christ: ". . . he likewise predestined us through Christ Jesus to be his adopted sons . . . that all might praise the glorious favor he has bestowed on us in his beloved" (Eph. 1:5,6). The incarnate Word is given to us as the model to be contemplated and reproduced. "Those whom he foreknew he predestined to share the image of his

Son . . ." (Rom. 8:29). That is our supernatural vocation: to grow like Jesus.

But, in the thought of God, Jesus and Mary are inseparable. One cannot be like Him, without being like her. The same eternal act which predestined Jesus to be our Saviour and model predestined Mary to be intimately united with Him in the whole mystery of redemption, and consequently to be, along with Him, the exemplar of our life. When the Lord forms His elect, He considers them not only in His incarnate Word, but also in her who is worthy to be called "mirror of justice," a pure reflection of His holiness. God wills us to become conformable to her image also.

Mary herself takes pains to impress that image on our soul. She is "the first agent of our redemption," says George of Venice. Just as the chief royal agent inscribed the officers on the prince's lists and put the seal to his sovereign decrees, Mary inscribes in the "book of life" those who are predestined by eternal Love and marks them with the seal of God. More than that, Blessed Hugh of Saint-Cher asserts that she is herself the "book of life" in which the Lord has written the names of the elect, in whom the Holy Spirit formed Christ and His members.

2. OUR LADY HAS MERITED GRACE FOR US

Our predestination begins to be accomplished through baptism, which by giving us grace makes us partakers of the intimate life of God. Baptism is our birth into the divine life.

Now this grace has been merited for us by Mary.

We must state clearly, first, that life comes to us from Jesus Christ, the one and only Saviour. The sacrifice of the Cross is the only cause, the total, necessary, and sufficient cause of our salvation. Not even the holiest of creatures could have redeemed us, whereas one drop of the blood of Jesus was enough to make superabundant atonement for our sins. If Providence had so decreed, the incarnate Word would have offered His sacrifice without the cooperation of any creature. Assuredly we should have been just as fully justified and sanctified, grace would have come down just as abundantly into our souls thus made children of God, and the stream of life would flow just as copiously.

But it pleased God to associate a Co-Redemptress with the Redeemer. "Just as in Adam, all die," says St. Paul, "so in Christ all will come to life again" (I Cor. 15:22). Eve, by her advice, had cooperated with the first man in our ruin. Mary by her consent cooperates with Christ in our salvation. There is an admirable unity in the divine plan. Woman contributes to our restoration as she had contributed to our fall.

We know well that the contribution of the new Eve adds nothing to the infinite riches of the sacrifice of the new Adam. Yet, in the Christian tradition, we love to recall that if Our Lord is the principal cause of our salvation, Our Lady is its secondary cause, and that the Mother has merited for us, congruously and through love, what the Son merited for us on strict grounds of justice. Their merit is of one order, since that of Mary depends entirely on that of Jesus. Both are universal — unlimited in the Co-Redemptress as in the Redeemer.

Far from being an offense to Thee, Lord Jesus, this

teaching glorifies the superabundance of Thy redemption, for from that alone the merit of Thy Mother draws all its power. We believe Thy sacrifice to be so perfect, so rich in grace, that it was able not only to save us, but to raise up beside Thee a Co-Redemptress who along with Thee could merit every grace for every man. Is not that the fairest fruit of Thy precious Blood?

a. THE ANNUNCIATION

God, by a free decree of His wisdom, had from eternity decided that the mystery of Christ would not be realized without the consent of her who, by her free acceptance, was to be ":the helper of the new Adam." Mary entered into that mystery as a cooperator, and truly merited grace for us. Her answer to God's messenger: *Ecce ancilla Domini, fiat mihi secundum verbum tuum,* does indeed express obedience, but still more it expresses resolution and authority. Until she has given her consent everything hangs in suspense. The eternal counsels will depend for their fulfillment on the "yes" that she can pronounce or withhold. Once it is spoken, the new supernatural order begins. Her humble fiat is mighty, boundless. We may compare it to the fiat of creation. The one made us men, the other makes us members of the incarnate Word, sons by adoption of God.

That fiat of Mary's is the sovereign act of her life. It brings Our Lady into the accomplishment of the divine mysteries. From now on the mystery of the Incarnation cannot unfold itself without her. Through her God is about to accomplish His great mystery, the mystery which redounds "unto the praise of the glory of His grace" (Eph. 1:6), the mystery of Christ, namely, Christ in us. When God decides to give Himself to creatures, He will do it through Mary, the intermediary between us and the divine life. The operations of union, of love, the diffusion of grace, will be performed by God through Mary.

Mary knew it. A prophetic light showed her the whole mystery of her Son, and she surrendered herself to it unreservedly. "She knows, she feels, she sees to what God is drawing, calling, raising her, and she enters into this divine state full of grace, of light, and of desire to serve God in this high ministry" (Cardinal Pierre de Berulle, *Vie de Jesus,* Ch. XV).

No doubt she did not know from that first moment the particular happenings, the secondary circumstances of the life of her Son, but she clearly saw what was essential in it, its principle and its goal. She knew, through the angel's words, not only that He was the "Son of the Most High," and that she would have the glory of being Mother of God, but that she would call Him "Jesus," that is, Saviour, and that she would have to give Him for the salvation of men. The great design of God, the diffusion of divine life through her Son, was apparent to her.

Can we doubt it? The whole of tradition asserts it. Our Lady assiduously read the Scriptures, the deep things of which the Holy Spirit revealed to her. She could not but know the great design so often announced by the prophets: the mysterious nuptials that the Lord intended to contract with human nature. "With age-old love I have loved you," so He spoke through the prophet Jeremiah (31:3); "so I have kept my mercy toward you." And

135

through Hosea (2:21-22): "I will espouse you to me forever: I will espouse you in right and in justice, in love and in mercy; I will espouse you in fidelity. . . ."

Our Lady penetrated the deep sense of these texts and of many others. She knew that the Messiah, her Son, would be the bridegroom of that mysterious marriage foretold in the Canticle. In her heart she already loved with the same love her Son and those with whom He was to be so closely united. If St. Paul, not long after, recognized so clearly that mystery of the union of Christ with His members, how brilliantly clear it must have been in the mind of Our Lady, who was to play such a decisive part in it! She saw, and she saw in an incomparably more perfect light, that her Son would be the Head of an immense body, and that the mystery of the Incarnation would not be completed in one instant in her womb, but would be accomplished little by little until the end of time by the formation of Christ's members of the Mystical Body.

She understood that as she was called to be the Mother of the Word incarnate, she must conceive Him in His totality, as St. Augustine was to express it, in the Head and in the members; and that her maternity would not reach its full perfection until she brought forth the whole Christ.

It was to the whole of this mystery that the Archangel, speaking for God, asked her consent, and Our Lady willed the whole of this mystery. At the same time that she accepted the motherhood of Jesus, she accepted the motherhood of the members of Jesus. From that day she was our mother. "My sweet Son Jesus is non *unigenitus,* an only Son," said Mary to St. Gertrude, "but *primogenitus,* my firstborn Son, because I conceived Him first in my womb. But after Him, or rather through Him, I conceived you all by adopting you into the innermost core of my motherheart, so that you might be at once my children and His brothers" (St. Gertrude, *The Herald of Divine Love,* Book IV: Ch. III).

"In the womb of His most pure mother Jesus Christ not only took mortal flesh, He also took a spiritual body, formed of all those who believe in Him. So that it can be said that Mary, bearing the Saviour in her womb, bore also all those whose life was included in His. Therefore, all of us, inasmuch as we are incorporated into Christ, are born of Mary's womb like the body united to the head. . . . In a spiritual and mystical but real way we are called children of Mary and she is the mother of us all" (Pius X, *Ad diem illum,* Feb. 2, 1904).

b. THE PRESENTATION

The heavenly Father had given Jesus to Mary. "Every child belongs to his mother, but no child in the same degree as Jesus to Mary, for she is unique in having conceived, formed, and brought forth her Son alone, with no human cooperation of any kind" (Msgr. C. L. Gay *Conference XXXV*). Jesus is her treasure, and she has all the right of a mother over Him.

But now the Lord reminded her by an inner light that she must give up her treasure, and that Jesus, the fruit of her womb and the supreme possession of her life, must become the possession of all, a common good, dedicated to the salvation of the world.

It was that sacrifice of her rights that the divine Mother accomplished when she presented her Son Jesus in the Temple. To submit humbly to the Law, to surrender her own self, was nothing more than the course of her everyday life. But now something much greater was asked of her: the sacrifice of her Son. Simeon was there to remind her of the great mystery of the Redemption: her Son was the Saviour and the Redeemer, He was to die for His brethren. Our Lady was to hand Him over to sacrifice, to death. She did it unhesitatingly, unreservedly, definitively. She abandoned her Son to the absolute rights of divine justice for the salvation of men. She give Him to be a victim. And she offered herself to go with Him wherever it should please Him to call her.

"They reach the altar," says St. Thomas of Villanova *(Sermon on the Purification of the Blessed Virgin Mary);* "the Virgin falls on her knees, burning with more fervent love than the seraphim in heaven. She has her Child in her arms. She offers Him to God as a sacrifice of most acceptable odour, with the prayer:

"O Almighty Father, accept the oblation that I Thy servant make to Thee for the whole universe. Take this Son who is ours: mine in time, Thine from all eternity. I give Thee boundless thanks for having raised me to the dignity of mother of Him whose Father Thou Thyself art. Take this most holy Victim from the hands of Thy servant. This is the morning offering which will one day on the arms of the Cross be the evening sacrifice. Good Father, look favorably on my offering, and consider for whom I am offering it to Thee."

It is true, Mary took her Son back with her to

Nazareth. She lived with Him in the sweet intimacy of family life. But we may be quite sure that the memory of Simeon's prophecy never left her, that she lived in the thought of Jesus' sacrifice, in the prospect of Calvary. The holy old man had held up the cross before her: her eyes were ever fixed on it. With all a mother's love, she busied herself about the divine Child and the adolescent, but she was as a priest preparing the victim for immolation. Like Abraham climbing up the mountain on which he was to immolate his son, Mary each day made one step towards Calvary.

Thus, on the day of the Presentation, she renewed her acceptance of the great mystery, consenting to sacrifice her Son for our salvation. It was because of us that she suffered.

c. CALVARY

Enlightened by a prophetic light, John the Baptist recognized in Jesus the Redeemer. He who would die to expiate the sins of men. "Look! There is the Lamb of God," he said, "who takes away the sin of the world!" (John 1:29).

How much more brilliantly clear that truth was in the eyes of Our Lady! Her perfect understanding of the divine Scriptures would have sufficed to reveal to her the fearful Passion towards which her Son was journeying. Did she not read in Isaiah this clear prophecy: "There was in him no stately bearing to make us look at him, nor appearance that would attract us to him. He was spurned and avoided by men, a man of suffering, accustomed to infirmity, One of those from whom men hide their faces, spurned, and we held him in no esteem" (Isaiah 53:2,3).

Mary read and meditated on these and other prophecies. She knew that they would be fulfilled in her Son. Doubtlessly, Jesus Himself often spoke of them with her as of the great work they had to accomplish in common. If He willed several times to announce to His disciples His Passion and Death at Jerusalem, how could He have been silent about them to His Mother, who was to have so important a share in them? He spoke of these things to her so that she might live with Him in the thought of the sacrifice, and that she might say like Him: "I have a baptism to receive. What anguish I feel till it is over!" (Luke 12:50).

Can we imagine what the thought of that terrible Passion meant to Our Lady and the presentiment of the cross that ever stood before the eye of her mind? Think of the agony of any other mother knowing beforehand the tortures that her child will have to endure. Then you will surmise something of Mary's inner martyrdom as she read in the Scripture verses like: "But he was pierced for our offenses, crushed for our sins . . . Like a lamb led to the slaughter . . . and opened not his mouth; . . . But the Lord was pleased to crush him in infirmity . . . and was counted among the wicked . . ." (Isaiah 53:5-12).

Blessed Angela of Foligno said of Jesus: "He abode in sorrow." The same might be said quite exactly of Our Lady, who felt each year, each day, that she was drawing nearer to the dreadful hour in which her Son would be handed over to the uttermost malice of men.

Now, it was for us that from the very first she accepted that martyrdom. The same prophecy that revealed to her the depth of the sufferings of her Son spoke to her also of their purpose, the salvation of men. "Yet it was our infirmities that he bore, our sufferings that he endured. . . . Upon him was the chastisement that makes us whole, by his stripes we were healed. . . . If he gives his life as an offering for sin, he shall see his descendants in a long life . . ." (Isaiah 53: 4,5,10).

Our Lady entered into God's designs, and accepted beforehand the sacrifice that would become a gushing fount of life. Although her heart was pierced, she longed, like Jesus, for the hour which was to give a "long-lived seed" to her Son and to herself and restore to God His lost children.

When that formidable hour had come, Mary was ready, and she stood erect by her Son's side: "Near the cross of Jesus there stood his mother . . ." (John 19:25).

"She stood," and like a sacrificing priest, she offered her victim freely, voluntarily. No creature can have any idea of her pain in those terrible hours, a pain made extreme by the ineffable tenderness of her heart, by the very fineness of her physical constitution and, above all, by her spiritual insight. She was both a mother and bound to her Son by a unique privilege of perfection and of holiness. And yet we must not think of her as overcome, fainting, supported by the holy women. No, *stabat,* she "stood," like the priest at the altar, absolute mistress of her thoughts, her feelings, and her will. She did more than submit to the demands of divine justice. She entered unreservedly into the designs of the eternal father, sacrificing her only Son for the salvation of the world. "She had to unite with the eternal Father and they had in common to deliver up to execution Him who was their Son in common, for that is why Providence called her to the foot of the cross" (Bossuet, *Sermon I on the Compassion*). She was implementing the consent spoken at the Annunciation, confirmed at the Presentation, renewed all her life long. She was giving her Son for us.

The dominant thought in her soul was the thought of our redemption. "When with her mother's eyes she looked fixedly at her Son's wounds," says St. Ambrose, "what was uppermost in her mind was not her beloved Son's death but the salvation of the world" (St. Ambrose, *Expositio Evangelii secundum Lucam*, Book X, No. 1532. J. P. Migne, *Patrologia Latina*, XV, 1837). If she could have taken Jesus down from the Cross and saved Him from death she would not have done it, any more than Jesus Himself willed to save Himself from His executioners. She, too, said in her heart: "Am I not to drink the cup the Father has given me?" (John 18:11). If all her life she was intimately united to her Son, willing all that He willed, never was that union more complete than in the hour in which Christ consummated His mission. "The will of Christ and that of Mary formed but one, their two holocausts formed but one. Jesus and Mary offered their sacrifice similarly to God: Jesus in the blood of His body, Mary in the blood of her heart" (Arnoldus Bonneval).

That is why Our Lady stood at the foot of the Cross, in the attitude of a priest, immolating her Son to give us life.

At the same time she offered herself, with her heart crushed and her soul in desolation, with her grief, "For deeper than the sea are her thoughts" (Sirach 24:27).

3. OUR LADY IS OUR MOTHER

We have shown that Mary twice became a mother. The first time at Bethlehem, in the expressible sweetness of supreme joy when the Word incarnate came into this world. The second time, on Calvary amidst indescribable anguish when a whole people came to the life divine. A mother is she from whom we have received life. I am born to grace through Our Lady. She is therefore truly my mother. I must not understand that name in a figurative sense, but in the most literal and real sense. Through a woman I received the life of the body, Mary has given me the life of the soul, the life that unites my immortal soul to God. She has loved me and suffered for me. Her heart, a heart overflowing with life, a woman's heart, a mother's heart, pours out its love on me. She is a perfect mother, possessing in its fullness and able to give out to me the divine life by which I must live. Her motherhood is in the image of God's fatherhood. She gives me everything with utter devotedness and affection. Since God has given her the office of distributing all His gifts to us, He has also charged her to do it with His love. That is her mission. It is not her function to teach or to judge. She loves, she is a mother.

She is so much a mother that wherever we see her exercising her divine maternity towards Jesus, we see her also exercising her maternity of grace towards us. At the crib she holds Jesus in her arms and presents Him to the shepherds and the Magi. In the Temple she offers Him, but it is for us. On Calvary she keeps watch by her Son and immolates Him for our salvation. It is at the moment that she is fulfilling her last maternal duty towards Jesus, that He announces her motherhood of souls.

4. OUR LADY IS MOTHER OF THE CHURCH

The power of her motherhood extends to the whole Church. Her mission was but beginning when she gave to Christ His material body. Now she gives Him His mystical body. From her body was formed the body of the Person of Christ. From her love, her active affection, is formed His Mystical Body. Jesus is only the first of her sons. She is, like Eve, "the mother of all the living" (Gen. 3:20). She seeks out the predestined to incorporate them into Christ. All who are predestined to grace are predestined to be her children.

Mary works to bring about the unity of souls in the Mystical Body. That is the work of her maternity. Through her is formed each mystical member of Jesus and in her all are united organically to the Head.

It was for the sake of the Church that Mary remained on earth after the Ascension. She performed for it the office she had already performed for Jesus. She watched over its cradle. The Scriptures have preserved for us the earliest vision of the Church. In one spirit, in prayer, the brethren of Jesus gathered about His mother. They needed her in order to preserve the spirit of Jesus and not to flinch when persecution began. The dangers that had beset the newborn Child of Bethlehem now beset His Mystical Body. The mother who saved the Christ Child had to be there to watch over the nascent Church. Is it not a striking thing that the mystery of Christ which could not begin at the Incarnation except through Mary, entered into its plenitude on the day of Pentecost, again through the mediation of and in the presence of Mary?

We invoke her every day by the title "Ark of the Covenant." The Ark of the Covenant in the Old Testament sheltered, in the silence of the Holy of Holies, the whole treasure of the faithful people, was their protection and their hope. Our Lady, acting always hiddenly, is at the wellspring of the life of the Church. As mothers do, she hides in the privacy of the home; but she distributes life. She is the Ark of the Covenant of the Church, its secret strength, the heart of its holiness.

5. THE IMMACULATE HEART OF MARY

Over and over again St. Paul explained to the early Christians that we live in Christ: *in Christo Jesu*. We are incorporated in Christ, baptized in Christ, clothed with Christ. Christ is the vital source of that supernatural life by which the members of His Mystical Body live. But just as Christ's human life was first brought into being in Mary's sacred womb, so our supernatural life is formed and brought into being through the agency and beneath the shadow and protection of the same Blessed Mother. So that we may say that we live, as it were, in Mary's womb. Is not Our Lady's maternal power also a sort of atmosphere in which Christendom lives? All the elect are formed in her spiritual womb. The life of grace is not, in its first beginnings, a perfect life. It has its movements of growth. It has its childhood. It is a life in process of formation. It needs a mother for the period of its weakness. And this period of childhood lasts the whole of our life on earth. As long as we are here we are in the period of childbirth, of formation. Even the saints are children in this respect. And see what intimacy with Our Lady comes of that, since we are being formed, as it were, in her womb. As long as the child lives in its mother's womb, it is one with her, it is dependent for the continuance of its life upon her. So all our life long Our Lady carries us in the warmth of her love. She feeds us with the grace of which she has the fullness.

Is there any fervent Catholic who does not feel that he is living and growing in the atmosphere of a mother's love?

"The Queen of grace and of mercy bent over her sons and daughters," Blessed Angela of Foligno tells us. "She bent down and blessed them with a vast blessing, and drawing them to her heart she embraced them unequally. It seemed as if her arms were the outstretched arms of love. She was entirely luminous and seemed to gather them into herself in endless light. Do not imagine that I saw her arms of flesh. She was wholly light, admirable light. The Blessed Virgin pressed her children to her heart, and by virtue of the love that flowed from her inmost being, absorbed them into herself" (Blessed Angela of Foligno, *Visions et Revelations*, Ch. XLVIII, Edit. Hello).

VI.

Our Lady Leads Us On to Perfection

1. GOD CALLS US TO HOLINESS

2. APPEAL TO MARY'S MOTHERHOOD

3. OUR LADY UNITES US WITH THE MYSTERIES OF CHRIST

4. OUR LADY UNITES US WITH THE SACRIFICE OF CHRIST
   a. OUR LADY'S UNION WITH CHRIST'S SACRIFICE
   b. OUR UNION WITH THE SACRIFICE THROUGH THE LITURGY
   c. OUR UNION WITH THE SACRIFICE IN DAILY LIFE

5. TO THE GLORY OF THE HOLY TRINITY
   a. OUR LADY UNITES US WITH THE FATHER
   b. OUR LADY UNITES US WITH THE WORD
   c. OUR LADY UNITES US WITH THE HOLY SPIRIT

ABANDONMENT TO OUR LADY

Our Lady Leads Us On to Perfection

1. GOD CALLS US TO HOLINESS

God chose us in Christ "before the world began, to be holy and blameless in his sight, to be full of love; he likewise predestined us through Christ Jesus to be his adopted sons . . . that all might praise the glorious favor he has bestowed on us. . ." (Eph. 1: 4-6).

That is our vocation. God calls us to share in His holiness by our adoption as sons in Christ. That is what St. Paul called the great mystery, "the mysterious design which for ages was hidden in God" (Eph. 3: 9), the mystery of the total Christ.

We know by faith the secret of the inner life of God. The Father has a Son equal to Him. Both are united in an embrace of infinite love whence the Holy Spirit proceeds. . . . The beatitude of the Father is to have a Son, "reflection of the Father's glory," says St. Paul (Heb. 1: 3).

But now God extends His fatherhood: He shares His beatitude with His creatures, drawn out of nothing but lifted up to Him by His pure goodness. He makes them His children. He "rescued us from the power of darkness and brought us into the kingdom of his beloved Son" (Col. 1: 13). That is the unimaginable grace of filial adoption. He adopts us in His beloved Son. From all eternity the Father looked with infinite satisfaction on the humanity united to the Word which would produce a rich flowering of holiness and love, not only in Christ the Redeemer, but in each of those that the Redeemer would unite with Himself: the Word incarnate leading His life of adoration and love in Himself and in His children by adoption. What astounding love! "See what love the Father has bestowed on us in letting us be called children of God!" (I John 3: 1).

In practice, holiness consists in becoming children of God through Christ: "Those whom he foreknew he predestined to share the image of his Son" (Rom. 8: 29). The Word became incarnate, "that we might receive our status as adopted sons" (Gal. 4: 5). He imparts the life of the Father to us and brings us into the divine family. Before our eyes He lived the life of a son. We must imitate Him. Our whole effort should be to unite with Jesus so as to share through Him in His filial life. There is no other means of going to God: "No one comes to the Father but through me" (John 14: 6). We must become sons of God in Jesus.

2. APPEAL TO MARY'S MOTHERHOOD

Since we are destined to become sons of God, let us appeal to Mary, Mother of the Firstborn. Her sovereign function is motherhood. She is daughter of the Father, Mother of the Word, Spouse of the Spirit. Has she not every title for introducing us into the family of God? She is the queen of the kingdom of grace.

We ask her to extend her motherhood to us. She formed the Head of the mystical Christ. So may she deign to form His members. May she spread as widely as God desires the Incarnation which began in her womb. May she watch over the growth of Christ's members as she watched over the growth of the Head. May she continue in us to be the mother of Christ. She must now bring to the perfection of their life the children whom she conceived at the Incarnation and brought to birth on Calvary: bring each, as St. Paul says: "and form that perfect man who is Christ come to full stature" (Eph. 4: 13). Our Lady can fulfill in us all that God wants of us. Her motherhood corresponds to the fatherhood of God. All our hopes of holiness rest in Mary's motherhood. She possesses and can give to us that "fullness of God" of which St. Paul spoke (Eph. 3: 19). You may aspire to enter, like her, into the overshadowing power of the Father and the action of the Holy Spirit. And of you will be born the Holy One who will be called the Son of God.

3. OUR LADY UNITES US WITH THE MYSTERIES OF CHRIST

The historical duration of Christ's mysteries is over but their operation remains. "Jesus Christ is the same yesterday," says St. Paul, "today, and forever" (Heb. 13: 8). Why did He "love the Church and deliver Himself for it"? In order to sanctify it. He did it during His earthly life by the mysteries of His sacred humanity. He does it still by those same mysteries, which are realities always active and sanctifying. They are an eternal reality. "Their power never ceases, nor will the love ever cease with which they were accomplished. The spirit, the state, the power, the merit, of the mystery is always present. The Spirit of God, for whom the mystery was performed; the inner state of the outward happening; the efficacity and the power which make the mystery alive and operative in us; that virtuous state and disposition, that merit by which He bought us for His Father and merited for us heaven, life, and Himself; even the actual delight, the eager disposition with which Jesus accomplished the mystery is still alive, actual, present to Jesus. So much so that if it were necessary, or pleasing to God His Father, He would be perfectly willing to suffer anew, and to accomplish anew the work, the action, the mystery. Therefore we must treat the things and the mysteries of Jesus not like things past and dead, but like things living and present and even eternal from which we have to gather precious eternal fruit" (Cardinal Pierre de Berulle, *Oeuvres*, p. 1052).

It is impossible to say how good it is for the soul to keep consciously united to the mysteries of Jesus, channels used by grace to give life to the world. That is the grace of the Rosary. The Rosary is Our Lady's means of uniting us to the ever-present mysteries of her Son, to the life-giving action of His humanity.

It is easy for her to lead us into that blessed world of the mysteries of Christ. They were accomplished in her presence; what is more, with her cooperation. She took an active part in them. They were events in her personal history at the same time as in her mission of motherhood. She grasped their marvellous economy and the connection of each with the sanctification of her children. She knows their fruitfulness because she always experienced it to the full. How can we conceive some idea of the union of Mary with Jesus in those mysteries? God worked an ineffable operation in her which makes one think of the inner life of the Trinity. "Jesus," says Berulle, "drew her into unity with Himself and out of her herself and her interior activity, so that she lived in Him; bearing up her holy aspirations by a kind of impression which was sweet, lofty, strong, and delightful, irresistibly drawing the Mother to the Son, the Virgin into Jesus." It was her whole life to contemplate the Word incarnate. "Mary's characteristic was to be intent on the inner spiritual life of her Son, to be pure capacity for Jesus, filled with Jesus."

She leads us into that world of mysteries by faith. Vital contact with Christ is established by faith, which is the opening of our intelligence to the hidden riches of Christ. It is perfected in charity. Because the apostles believed in Jesus the Father loved them: "The Father already loves you, because you have loved me and have believed that I came from God" (John 16: 27). That faith draws down grace. Jesus said: "He who believes in me . . . From within him rivers of living water shall flow" (John 7: 38). Through it we attain to divine sonship.

Now, Our Lady is called *Virgo fidelis,* the Virgin of faith, by the Church. Faith in the angel's word, though he announced an unimaginable mystery, gave her entrance into the mystery of Christ, that mystery which God, as St. Paul says, had kept hidden from eternity. Those novel secrets of the Trinity, the Incarnation, the Mystical Body, how did Mary learn of them but from the word of God's messenger? "Blest is she who trusted that the Lord's words to her would be fulfilled" (Luke 1: 45), said her cousin to her. When she accepted the message in faith she entered into the fulfillment of God's greatest designs. The Word would live in her because of her faith. All her love for her Son rested on that unshakeable faith which God subjected to such terrible trials. Her pure simple faith made her the handmaid of the Lord.

May Christ "dwell in your hearts through faith . . . may charity be the root and foundation of your life" (Eph. 3: 17). That faith and charity bind us to Christ and at last make ours the mysteries that He lived for us. As St. Paul says: "God is rich in mercy; because of His great love for us he brought us to life with Christ. Both with and in Christ Jesus he raised us up and gave us a place in the heavens, that in the ages to come he might display the great wealth of his favor, manifested by his kindness to us in Christ Jesus" (Eph. 2: 4-7). We live again through all the mysteries of Jesus: nailed to the Cross with Him, buried with Him, risen along with Him. St. Paul writes (Gal. 2: 19): "I have been crucified with Christ"; and (Col. 2: 12): "You were not only buried with him but also raised to life with him because you believed in the power of God." By reliving the mysteries of Jesus, "he predestined us to share the image of his Son" (Rom. 8: 29).

"O Jesus, living in Mary, come and live in Thy servants, in the spirit of Thy holiness, in the fulness of Thy strength, in the perfection of Thy ways, in the truth of Thy virtues, in the communion of Thy mysteries victorious over every adverse power, in Thy Spirit, for the Glory of Thy Father" (M. Olier).

4. OUR LADY UNITES US WITH THE SACRIFICE OF CHRIST

a. OUR LADY'S UNION WITH CHRIST'S SACRIFICE

Jesus lived with the Cross before His eyes. He ever walked towards Calvary. He was the Saviour of the world and the idea of His sacrifice never left Him for a moment. To understand His life one must look at it in the light of His death. From the moment of His entry into the world He said to God: "Sacrifice and offering you did not desire, but a body you have prepared for me. . . . I have come to do your will" (Heb. 10: 5-7). That sacrifice, first offered in Mary's womb, was to be continued for thirty-three years, until Jesus said: "Now it is finished" (John 19: 30).

Like Jesus, Mary was dedicated to the Cross. The grace of her divine motherhood as well as her unique love required it. Because she was mother of God she received a singular grace, exceeding by far all the gifts received by the other children of adoption: a grace of affinity, placing her as Cajetan says, "within the confines of divinity." In that Our Lady found her cross. She was to resemble the Redeemer as closely as possible. The grace of being foremost daughter of adoption modelled her on Jesus, especially in His love of the cross. She was foremost in cross-bearing, because she was foremost in grace. And also because she was foremost in love. "When love is boundless," says St. Albert the Great, "suffering is also boundless" (St. Albert the Great, *Super missus*, q. 78).

"There is no love comparable to Mary's," says Richard of St. Lawrence, "and therefore no suffering equalled her suffering" (Richard of St. Lawrence, In *Cantica Canticorum*, Ch. XXVI). Her martyrdom came from the excess of her love.

Jesus gave her a share in His terrible secret. It was not possible that Jesus should live in the cruel foresight of Calvary and Mary, beside Him, lead a tranquil life. The love between them demanded the closest union. It was through love that Jesus gave Mary a share in his cross-freighted destiny. His sacrifice, His Passion, was the crowning point in His life.

Love required Him to lead His mother up to it with Him. She was His mother. Without a part in His suffering, would she have been anything more than an instrument?

Besides, if Jesus had not first offered Mary a share in His sacrifice, Mary would have asked for it so humbly and so ardently that her love would have obtained it. If she longed to follow Jesus everywhere, she longed above all to follow Him where He was to suffer. She wanted, in the words of Jesus (Matt. 20: 22), to drink of His chalice. The greatest gift of Jesus to Mary was her own compassion, that compassion which enabled her to suffer with Him, to sacrifice herself with Him, to glorify God and to exercise her motherhood of men. Was she not, moreover, the principle of the Passion, as St. Augustine gives us to understand, when she gave to her Son the nature which alone would enable Him to suffer?

In order to understand the life of Our Lady we must look at it, as we must look at the life of Jesus, in the light of the Cross. Enlightened, from the moment of the Incarnation, about the deep sense of the prophecies, and warned later by the venerable Simeon, she lived in the thought of the great sacrifice to come. After the words of the holy man, she knew that she was going to live with a victim, in order to prepare Him for the sacrifice. Thenceforward the Passion was always before her. Everything reminded her of what had been foretold. She herself said to St. Bridget: "Every time that I saw my Son, that I wrapped Him in swaddling clothes, that I looked at His hands and His feet, every time was my soul pierced as it were afresh by another sword of sorrow. I seemed to see Him already crucified" (*Revelations,* Book VI, Ch. LVII). Our Lord revealed it to St. Teresa:

"When thou seest My mother holding Me in her arms, do not imagine that her joys were unaccompanied by cruel torment. From the moment that she heard Simeon's words, My Father showed her by a vivid light what I should have to suffer" (Edition of the Paris Carmelites, Vol. II, p. 247). "What a prolonged martyrdom thou didst endure," says Rupert, "thou didst always foresee how thy Son would die" (Rupert, in *Cantica Canticorum,* Book III). He puts the following words on Mary's lips: "Beware of limiting thy compassion for me to the hour that I saw my Son die. Simeon's sword pierced me all my life. When my Son was in my arms, when I suckled Him, I already saw His death. What a long-drawn out torture I endured!" (Ibid). "No, my sweet Queen," said St. Anselm, "I do not believe that thou couldst live for one single moment in the embrace of such sorrow if the Spirit of life had not supported thee" (St. Anselm, *De excellent. Vir.,* Ch. V).

When the day of the supreme sacrifice drew near, Our Lady came to the Holy City. She too might have said: "I have a baptism to receive. What anguish I feel till it is over!" (Luke 12: 50). She knew that her Son's sacrifice would inaugurate the kingdom of God, that from His blood would be born sons of God. She knew that her Son was "the grain of wheat falling into the earth" (of her womb), which, unless it die, "it remains just a grain of wheat. But if it dies, it produces much fruit" (John 12: 24). She saw all the predestined who would be born of the sacrifice of Calvary, the multitude of children of God born in the suffering of Calvary. Her love urged her. When the day came, she was on Calvary.

Immense love drew her there. She stood at the foot of the Cross: stood in the face of suffering, because she dominated it. In mind and heart she shared all her Son's torments. She was wholly united and, as it were, identified with Him, so intensely did she will with Him the same will of God, so utterly did she follow it out to the end with absolute self-surrender. She sacrificed her Son of us. On Calvary above all she gave us Jesus. Like God the Father, she so loved us that she gave us her only Son.

b. OUR UNION WITH THE SACRIFICE THROUGH THE LITURGY

It is absolutely necessary that we should unite with the sacrifice of Christ. That sacrifice, "the source of eternal salvation" (Heb. 5: 9), will only be fully efficacious if in mind, in heart, in our actions, we take an active part in it. Through union with the Passion we can fulfill our Christian vocation, for all graces come from the Cross. Jesus died to make us holy. "Christ loved the Church. He gave himself up for her . . . to present to himself a glorious Church, holy and immaculate, without stain or wrinkle or anything of that sort" (Eph. 5: 25-27).

Thus we understand why Our Lady brings us to the foot of the Cross. There flows the spring of holiness. Those who unite with Christ's oblation are sanctified: "By one offering he has forever perfected those who are being sanctified" (Heb. 10: 14).

We have two principal means of uniting with the Passion of Christ: the liturgy· and the acceptance of the sufferings of our daily life.

The altar perpetuates Calvary. In order that the graces of His death may be applied to all men in every age, Jesus unceasingly renews His sacrifice. He continues to be priest and victim.

At the communion He comes as priest. A priest's office is to adore and expiate. Within us He gives God perfect adoration, complete thanksgiving. He brings down pardon and divine grace. Within us, He adores, loves, thanks, makes reparation, pleads. All these acts of the eternal High Priest, which are done in us, become ours if we will. We may make our own all Christ's adoration, love, expiation, supplication and thanksgiving. The interior movement which bore Jesus towards His Father can become the interior movement of our life. We can render the most perfect homage to God, as the liturgy says: "By Him and with Him and in Him be to Thee, Almighty Father, all honor and glory in the unity of the Holy Spirit."

Jesus comes also as a victim, in His state of immolation. He comes as sacrificial victim, with the holiness if we may put it so of the Christ-Victim. The sacrificial host is kept apart from every profane contact, reserved, consecrated to God. According to St. Thomas, the marks of living holiness are freedom of affection from earthly things by purity and firm adhesion to God. The liturgy makes us share in the sublime holiness of Christ on the cross, where He was moved by pure love of His Father, where He was "an offering to God, a gift of pleasing fragrance" (Eph. 5: 2).

What a source of grace for the Christian who truly takes part in the Mass! He pays to God the most perfect homage of filial adoration. He draws directly from the wellspring of all grace. He intensifies his inner life by contact with the death of Christ. Little by little he becomes a living victim offered every day with the victim of Calvary. The Christian vocation is fulfilled.

But how could we take part in the sacrifice without remembering and invoking the Mother of the High Priest and of the Victim? Our Lady shared too intimately in her Son's priesthood during their earthly life not to be linked for ever with the exercise of that priesthood. As she was present on Calvary, she is present at Mass, which is a prolongation of Calvary. At the foot of the Cross, she stood by her Son as He offered Himself to the Father. At the altar she stands by the Church, the Mystical Body of Christ, as it offers itself with its Head renewing His sacrifice. Let us offer Jesus through Our Lady. Mary is the Mother of our Priest-Victim.

But Jesus does not want to be offered alone. The Mass is the sacrifice of Christ, but it is also the sacrifice of Christ's mystical members, of the Church. It involves essentially the offering of Christ's mystical members, immolated with Him in the same sacrifice and in the same sentiments of self-abandonment and complete submission. When the priest offers the host to God, let Him also offer our immortal soul, our body, our whole life, as St. Paul tells us to do: "I beg you . . . offer your bodies as a living sacrifice holy and acceptable to God" (Rom. 12: 1). Let this offering be made through Our Lady.

We must ask Mary to raise up servants formed in that liturgical spirit, who will be able, for the glory of God, to draw on the boundless resources of the liturgy, and more especially of the Mass. The value of the Mass is in itself boundless, but the servants of God have to use it, to appropriate it in their approach to God. In the first years of the Church, when Our Lady was still alive, she gave to the Masses celebrated by the apostles an efficacy of which we may judge by the vigorous growth of the Church in those blessed times. It is the saints who make the blood of Christ on our altars eloquent and efficacious with His Father.

c. OUR UNION WITH THE SACRIFICE IN DAILY LIFE

That union of thought, heart, and prayer with the sacrifice of Christ through the liturgy must be completed by the union with it of the actions of our daily life. St. Paul wrote to the Romans: "Are you not aware that we who were baptized into Christ Jesus were baptized into his death? Through baptism into his death we were buried with him (6: 3-4). . . . "Our old self was crucified with him" (6:6). He said to the Galatians (2: 19): "I have been crucified with Christ."

These words are exceptionally grace-laden. They must guide our life. The grace of baptism has fashioned us after our Saviour, has made us sharers in His death: a grace which is not isolated, but a seed that must germinate and fructify. Each Christian must reproduce the Passion and, like St. Paul, be nailed to the Cross. "In the same way," since you are baptized, "you must consider yourselves dead to sin but alive for God in Christ Jesus" (Rom. 6: 11).

Christ Himself had warned us: "Whoever wishes to be my follower must deny his very self, take up his cross each day" (Luke 9: 23). Let us love the Cross in its various forms: trials, work, sickness, humiliations, and everything else; everything that Providence sends us, the sooner to make us resemble Christ. To these things we must all add the voluntary labor of mortification and penance, a baptismal engagement from which there is no dispensation.

When the hour comes of union with the sacrifice of Christ, nothing will help us more than to think of her who suffered so much for us. She suffered all her life. The law of sacrifice enveloped her. Her suffering itself grew constantly, for suffering and love grow side by side in predestined souls. She suffered in her body, but above all in her heart and soul. Hers was above all an interior martyrdom.

Days will come when physical pain grips us relentlessly. Then we must remember that we are members of Christ and that it is our vocation to continue His passion. Before us, Our Lady travelled by that royal road of the Cross. Think of her exile, her poverty, her loneliness. In whatever condition we are, even though it be extreme and beyond relief, we must ever see Our Lord and Our Lady bearing the same cross before us and even heavier crosses.

Grief of heart is more terrible, but it is also more profitable. How searching are separations, mental torture, sadness even unto death! Then, above all, we must look at Mary. She suffered more in her heart than in her body. The intensity of her union with her Son increased her pain indescribably. She would have suffered less had she loved less. She suffered alone. He who could have consoled her, the only one who understood her grief, Jesus, was precisely the principal cause of her agony. She had to suffer without sympathy, a terrible thing.

She teaches us to suffer for Jesus. "I have been crucified with Christ" (Gal. 2: 19), said St. Paul. It was far truer of Mary. She was associated with the work of redemption and her motherhood made her enter into it more deeply than anyone. It is not enough to say that her sympathy made her feel the pain of her Son's sufferings. She entered into that pain, made it her own, identified herself with it. In truth there was only one Passion, endured at the same time by the Son and the Mother. Our Lady said that to St. Bridget: "In His Passion, His pain was my pain, because His heart was my heart" (*Revelations,* Book VII, Ch. XXXV). As she had given her body at the Incarnation so that the Word could take our nature in her womb, unstintingly she gave her body, her heart, her soul, on Calvary, to endure the martyrdom that redeemed us. She suffered to establish the kingdom of God on earth. She was thinking of us. The mother was suffering: the mother of Jesus, but also the mother of His brethren, the mother of mercy, the mother of the Mystical Body, the advocate of sinners. One cannot discover the least motion of indignation in the Passion. Her Son delivered Himself up to God's justice, but invoked pardon for those who crucified Him. His mother did the same. Her Son's executioners were also her children. Can you understand the fierce pain? The child of her virginal flesh, Jesus, put to death by those to whom, with ineffable love, she was giving birth in her heart!

"Your mother's birthpangs forget not" (Sirach 7: 27), Holy Scripture tells us. Our Lady wants to unite us with the Passion of her Son. We were a part of the Passion. In the immolation of Christ we were not spectators, but active sharers and in truth executioners. It was through our sins that Christ died and that Mary endured that dreadful martyrdom.

Our Lady desires us again in our day to have a share in the Passion, but through love now, and as St. Paul says, "fill up what is lacking in the sufferings of Christ" (Col. 1: 24). In our flesh we too must have our compassion for the sorrows of the Redeemer, compassion through the union of faith and love, through the action of penance and pain. That is the condition of our salvation: "heirs of God, heirs with

Christ, if only we suffer with him" (Rom. 8: 17).

We must continue the redeeming work of Christ. The Church lives by His sacrifice. That sacrifice is renewed every day on the altar, but it is also continued in the suffering members of Jesus. The suffering of Christians is necessary for the salvation of the world. It is a source of life. It expiates, redeems, sanctifies.

When God does us the honor of calling us to suffer, let us be glad. Jesus gives Himself to us in all His mysteries but nowhere so much as in the mystery of the Cross. There are exchanges of love that take place in suffering. It was on Calvary that Jesus gave His mother to John. "For it is your special privilege to take Christ's part—not only to believe in him but also to suffer for him" (Phil. 1: 29).

Our Lady teaches us to suffer in silence, hiddenly. Silence is the atmosphere of pain. There was silence on Calvary. We lose all that is most sanctifying in suffering by complaining, by talking of our troubles, by seeking consolation. Do not waste this precious grace.

Do you understand the union of the suffering soul with God? He who lives in the spirit of sacrifice does more than follow Jesus, he enters into the heart of His mystery. He can say with St. Paul: "and the life I live now is not my own; Christ is living in me" (Gal. 2: 20). Jesus said to Blessed Angela of Foligno: "Those who love and follow the way I followed, the way of sorrows, are My legitimate children. Those whose inner eye is fixed on My Passion and death, on My death which is the life and salvation of the world, on My death and not on other things, are my legitimate children. And the others are not" *(Vie et revelations,* Ch. XXXIII).

With the liturgy, let us ask Our Lady to give us that spirit of sacrifice, to be immolated with her Son:

"Holy Mother, pierce me through,
In my heart each wound renew
Of my Saviour crucified."

5. TO THE GLORY OF THE HOLY TRINITY

The essence of the inner life is devotion to the Holy Trinity. It is absolutely necessary to foster special sentiments of devotion for each of the Three Persons: filial love for the Father who gave us His only-begotten Son; entire and utter trust in the Word, our Redeemer and universal Mediator; self-surrender to the Holy Spirit dwelling in our souls, our guide, our master, our giver of gifts in the spiritual life.

Holiness is the inexpressible union of God with Himself in the Trinity of Persons. That infinite mutual clinging of Father and Son in the unity of the Holy Spirit, that movement of love consummating Their unity and crowning Their beatitude which causes God to find all His felicity in Himself, in His nature, and in the union of the Three Persons: that is the divine holiness. God is holy because the perfection of His nature separates Him infinitely from what is not Himself and because He is infinitely happy in the living embrace of the Three Persons together.

Similarly, Our Lady is holy. Her incommunicable name is *Sancta Maria,* Holy Mary, the holy virgin. She is holy because she is a virgin. Virginity is integrity, absence of division. She is holy because, being established in God at her creation, she never sought to cling to anything outside God, because she lived in God, entirely turned towards God.

For us holiness can only be imitation of that holiness of God: to cling to God with our intelligence, our will and in our external actions so as to be, as St. Paul says, "one and the same spirit" (I Cor. 12: 11) with Him. Holiness means reducing all things to one, needing only God.

Who will lead us to that crowning-point of our life? Once more, Our Lady. By her virginity she is the singularly beloved daughter of the Father: she will introduce us into the divine adoption, through her we shall become God's children. By her divine motherhood, she is the mother of the only-begotten Son of God. She will make us brothers of her firstborn. By her human motherhood she is the bride of the Holy Spirit: through her we shall enter the Mystical Body, the graces of the Redemption will flow from her to us.

a. OUR LADY UNITES US WITH THE FATHER

Mary is the supremely privileged daughter of the Father. God endowed Mary with all the beauty He could bring together in one creature. He willed the plenitude of nature and grace to meet in a creature who was only a creature, who would manifest the primal idea of God in creation: and He created the mother of His Son. She received more gifts than all angels and men together. God united and surpassed in the formation of the mother of His Son all the splendor that he had brought together in the angelic creation, all the life and power that He had bestowed in creating men. She, alone, is "full of grace." That says everything. In her you can read, more than in all other creatures, the power and love of God. She is the mirror of the Invisible, in as far as a creature can be.

The liturgy tells us that the purpose of the Incarnation was to bring us to the love of the invisible Father through the knowledge of the Son made visible in the flesh. God was not to remain in light inaccessible. He who is our life, our light, was to come within human reach. And so He manifested Himself first in the Word incarnate, and then in Mary: in Jesus, God in the midst of us; in Mary, the ideal form of the creature united with God. So we can see in Jesus what God is for us; in Mary what He wants us to be for Him.

This creation of Mary in the glory of virginity and grace already made her a singular object of the good pleasure of the Father. But their intimacy was unimaginably deepened when Our Lady gave birth to the Word. Here speech is powerless. "To establish an eternal alliance with thee," says Bossuet, "He willed thee to be the mother of His only-begotten Son, and Himself to be the Father of thine. O marvel! O abyss of charity! What mind would not be lost in contemplation of the incomprehensible marks of His delight in Thee, from the moment that thou camest so near to Him through your common Son, the invisible bond of your holy alliance, the pledge of your mutual attachment so lovingly given by each to the other." "Our common Son!" God the Father and Mary meet in a common center of love, in Jesus their only-begotten Son. They proclaim in ineffable union: "What is mine is thine." Only the union of the Three Divine Persons surpasses the union of the Father and the Blessed Virgin. "These two sacred persons, the Father who is in heaven and the mother who is on earth, are now bound together, and they too have as the bond of their holy union a divine Person, one Son, only-begotten, proceeding from them, who is between them the indissoluble bond to whom they are united for eternity" (Cardinal Pierre de Berulle).

That union was to go still further: Our Lady's motherhood was to go as far as God's fatherhood of men. As she was mother of the Son by nature, so she became mother of the children by adoption. God has children, but it is through her. If grace gives children to the Father, does He not owe them to Our Lady? The Incarnation and Mary's fiat were necessary to form the Mystical Body of Christ.

The consequence of this is easy to conjecture. It is through Our Lady, our mother in grace, that we shall learn to act as sons of God.

Our whole supernatural life rests on the eternal sonship of the Word. Our sonship by adoption, St. Thomas tells us, is assimilation to the sonship of the eternal Word and makes us share in the unity of the Word with His Father. That is the basis of our supernatural state. But our actions must flow from that state. We must live, pray, work, suffer, as children of God. "Be imitators of God as his dear children" (Eph. 5: 1). "Walk. . . . while you have the light" (John 12: 35, 36). "When you pray, say 'Father'" (Luke 11: 2).

The Father embraces with one embrace of love His only-begotten Son and His children of adoption. "He who loves me will be loved by my Father. . . The Father already loves you because you have loved me and have believed that I came from God" (John 14: 21; 16: 27). The eternal love of the Father for His Son flows down at the same time on His children of adoption. Jesus tells us: "I have given them the glory you gave me that they may be one, as we are one—I living in them, you living in me—that their unity may be complete. So shall the world know that you sent me, and that you loved them as you loved me" (John 17: 22, 23).

The essential duty of the Christian therefore is to be in everything the child of God. Let us call on Mary's motherhood. Her sovereign mission is to form the children to God. The greatest happiness that we can give her is to let her bring us to the birth of grace. May she give us the sense of sonship, to love the Father and to speak to Him like children.

b. OUR LADY UNITES US WITH THE WORD

Who could describe the union of Mary with Jesus? God alone can understand it. At the moment of the Incarnation, Mary gave the purest of her blood in the formation of the body of the Word. With what love she gave it! The Son of God responded by a love greater still. He gave her an immense grace, His divine life. He became wholly hers. With unique predilection the Trinity had formed the heart of the Blessed Virgin, that she might be the mother of the Word incarnate and love, fittingly, the Man-God. That union constantly increased during the earthly life of Jesus. Think of the union springing from the life at Nazareth, work in common, poverty borne together, the same boundless desire for the salvation of men.

There were unimaginable exchanges: from Jesus to Mary flowed graces of light, an unbroken revelation so to say of the divine mysteries; from Mary to Jesus, perfect adaptation to those graces, admirable docility to every inspiration, the full flowering of love. Think above all of their union on Calvary, when a common will made them accept the astounding sacrifice.

"In speaking of thee, Mary, we speak of Jesus. Speaking of thy dispositions, we speak of those in which He was to be born. Thou art His, thou art through Him, thou art for Him. And as the divine Persons subsist in the Trinity only through their mutual relations, thou also, O holy Virgin, O person at once divine and human, divine by grace and human by nature, thou dost subsist in the being of grace only through thy relation to Jesus. Thou didst live only by His grace before He lived to thee by nature. Thou breathest only by His Spirit, and thy graces and glories are His" (Cardinal Pierre de Berulle).

We can understand that that ineffable union enables Our Lady to unite us with Jesus. That union with Jesus Christ is the goal that St. Paul continually sets for our spiritual life: "For, to me, 'life' means Christ" (Phil. 1: 21).

Who will give us Christ? The Father. But He does it through Mary. Our Lady reveals Jesus to us. She teaches us to contemplate Him. Did she not spend her whole life in that contemplation? We cannot think without a kind of inner dazzlement of that interior life of Our Lady, looking at Jesus with her mother love and her boundless faith. The actions of Jesus, His words, were every one of them like a new revelation to Mary. Every motion of Jesus set up in her a deep, inner vibration giving rise to acts of perfect love.

The liturgy often invites us to ask Our Lady to reveal her Son to us: "Show us the blessed fruit of thy womb, Jesus." This knowledge of Jesus is indeed the starting point of love. The charity of Christ is then revealed to us, the charity which made Him our brother.

"The love of Christ impels us" (II Cor. 5: 14), as the Apostle says. It urges us to live like Jesus, to suffer like Jesus, to continue His work in the Church. What is the whole Christian life but the continuation of the life of Jesus by the practice of the same virtues? Christ extends His life in me by grace. It is my life, but it is also His: "And the life I live now is not my own; Christ is living in me" (Gal. 2: 20). Glory is given to God: "All these are yours, and you are Christ's, and Christ is God's" (I Cor. 3: 22-23).

c. OUR LADY UNITES US WITH THE HOLY SPIRIT

"The Holy Spirit will come upon thee," said the angel to Our Lady. He had already come at her first sanctification, at the moment of Mary's creation, her Immaculate Conception. "Hail, full of grace," said the angel. Every grace that a creature can receive she had already received to the full capacity of her being. Nothing was refused her of the gifts of God. The Blessed Trinity created a soul capable of receiving all Its gifts, in which It would find unique joy and a great object of glory. The Holy Spirit had so to say taken possession of Mary from the moment of her creation and had inundated her with divine life to prepare her to receive the Word. It was He who now made Mary fruitful. He formed in her the body of the Word: "The Holy Spirit will come upon you . . . hence the holy offspring to be born will be called Son of God" (Luke 1: 35).

Since then it has been always so. The Holy Spirit

continues to form the Mystical Body of Christ. He does it through Mary. The formation of the saints is their common work. That tells us what the union of Our Lady with the Holy Spirit really is. The Holy Spirit shows her the vocation of each of Christ's members, the degree of glory each is to obtain, his present dangers, the graces he needs. The whole plan of predestination is known to her: she fulfills it. Since no grace is given to any soul without Mary's mediation, it is a sign that the Holy Spirit reveals the condition of the Mystical Body to her and gives her the task of furthering its progress. What a union is this ever-present collaboration of the Holy Spirit and Our Lady in the formation of Christ! Together they produce Jesus in the Church. They produce Him in me. Wherever Jesus is born it is as it was the first time. He is born of the Holy Spirit and Mary.

Our Lady draws the Holy Spirit down into us: "When the Holy Spirit finds Mary in a soul," says St. Louis Mary Grignion de Montfort, "He flies thither, He enters fully, He communicates Himself abundantly to that soul in as far as it makes room for the spouse. And one of the great reasons why the Holy Spirit does not now work striking wonders in souls is that He does not find in them a close enough union with His faithful and inseparable spouse."

By that active presence of the Holy Spirit, we complete our entrance into the divine family. He reveals Jesus to us as Jesus foretold. He gives us the sense of sonship. You have received: "a spirit of adoption through which we cry out, 'Abba!' Father!'" (Rom. 8: 15). It is the Spirit of Jesus: "You are sons . . . God has sent forth into our hearts the spirit of his Son" (Gal. 4: 6). This Spirit acts in us, directs our activity, as He directed the human activity of Jesus and as He directs the Church: "All who are led by the Spirit of God are sons of God," says St. Paul (Rom. 8: 14). So that we can pray like children: "The Spirit too helps us in our weakness, for we do do not know how to pray as we ought; but the Spirit himself makes intercession for us with groanings which cannot be expressed in speech" (Rom. 8: 26).

ABANDONMENT TO OUR LADY

From these reflections let us conclude that we must abandon ourselves to Mary. We know her love for us. We know her power. She has light to guide us, goodness, grace. Let us trust ourselves to her, hope in her, accept the influence of her mother love.

To abandon oneself means in the first place to give oneself to her. But it means more than that. It means to lay self aside, to forget oneself, to surrender oneself unreservedly. It is true that in the last resort it is to God that one is abandoning oneself, for His fatherly will alone governs the world and especially the spiritual world. But we reach the perfection of abandonment to God by abandonment to Our Lady. Is she not closely associated with the government of the spiritual world? Her position as mother and queen is a real and active royalty. She forms the saints. God has conceived the idea of my spiritual life, of my life in Christ. He entrusts its realization to Our Lady. She holds the thread of all the events which Providence uses to make me a member of Christ, one of the elect. St. John tells us: "We have come to know and to believe in the love God has for us" (I John 4: 16). Consequently, I have only to believe, to hope, to let myself be molded.

Let us place in Mary's hands all that is ours, body and immortal soul, sensibility, imagination, intelligence, free will, merits. Let all these things be in her power. Let her direct our thoughts and desires, let her govern all our activity. Let us be really hers in order to be entirely God's.

Spiritual writers are wont to say that to practice this abandonment to Our Lady, the simplest way is to live with her, through her, and in her.

To live "with" Mary is easy when one loves her. By the intuitions of faith, we enter into communication with our mother and model. To pray, work, suffer, with her, changes life. It is association, continuous cooperation, with the Immaculate. Before us, she reached the perfection that we must reach. Wherever we go, however arduous our path, whatever cross we carry, let us look and we shall see Our Lady before us.

You who have the happiness of having served God for a long time, look at her. She too is the splendor of God, the revelation of the beauty of God. The nobility that the Lord wants to make conspicuous in Christ's members, the humility, purity, faith, charity, are living in the Blessed Virgin, so humble and so great, so loving and so strong.

And you, sinners, weak in faith, impure, proud, do you too live with her. She is so humanly compassionate, so sensitive to sorrow. However wretched you are, and because you are wretched, look at your mother.

She is always with us by her enveloping love; with us by the graces she distributes; with us by her prayer which is our strength; with us by her example which exhorts us; with us even when we do not think of her, for she is always thinking of us, as a mother of

174

her children, in joy and sorrow, "now and at the hour of our death," as every day we ask her to think of us. It is a companionship of influence and love. We can say with Elizabeth: "Whence is this to me that the mother of my Lord should come to me?"

We must live "through" Our Lady: she is our Mediatrix, *Janua coeli*, gate of heaven, gate of grace. Through her, Christ comes to us, through her we go to Christ. She helps our prayer. She tempers what in the Godhead might overwhelm us. She is the "mirror of justice," and of divine holiness, she makes the divine perfection more accessible. Hope of holiness and of heaven becomes easier for us through her. She supplies by her Son's merits and her own what was wanting in our actions and petitions. We offer our prayers and our work through her. It seems as if she said to us, like her Son, "For these I pray" (John 17: 9). Rising from a heart that lacks fervor, our poor prayer has the good fortune to meet Mary's prayer, which takes hold of it, wraps it in love, and makes it hers. It becomes the prayer of mother and children and goes up to the throne of God.

To live through Mary is to forget self, to be detached from self. One of the principal obstacles to the spiritual life is that preoccupation with self which makes us forget God's views, which prevents us from clearly seeing into the designs of Divine Providence. To renounce our own conceits and adapt ourselves to Our Lady's views is to enter into the accomplishment of the divine designs. For that is needed interior silence which makes us docile and flexible to God's leading. It is impossible to express how rapidly those souls advance, whom self-forgetfulness makes docile to Our Lady's inspiration, or to describe the inner peace they enjoy. Abandonment to Our Lady has delivered them from their own judgment in the direction of their lives and therefore from the illusions of sensibility and pride. Now Our Lady gently and strongly directs their efforts, their prayers, their thoughts. She is truly the Queen who reigns with motherly but powerful majesty. The soul enters deeply into the intimacy of God.

To live "in" Mary, under her constant influence, in dependence on her and, as it were, clinging to her, having "the same heart and mind"; to make her intentions ours; to pray as she in the same spirit of humility and adoration, to unite with her religious reverence, her love; to become, as St. Louis Mary Grignion de Montfort says, "living copies of Mary"; it is a great gift to reach that intimacy with the Mother of God. It is the most direct means of living in Christ. It is in Our Lady that we shall find the life of Christ ready to be shared with us. "I implore you," said M. Olier, "to withdraw often into the divine inner life of Mary whom God set up as mediatrix of the sacred gift of His Son to the Church. In that sanctuary you will find movements of adoration, praise, and love of God a thousand times more august than any that will ever be offered Him by creation. . . . For that reason I continue to implore you to go to that divine sanctuary, because in union with the Blessed Virgin you will make more progress for God and for the Church and for yourselves, than by any other practices that you could adopt."

"O holy Virgin, Mother of God, Queen of men and of angels, marvel of heaven and of earth, I revere thee in every way that I can according to God. I revere thee as I ought according to thy greatness and as the only-begotten Son, Jesus Christ Our Lord, wishes thee to be revered on earth and in heaven.

"I offer thee my soul and my life. I desire to belong to thee for ever and to pay thee some special homage and mark of dependence in time and eternity. Mother of grace and mercy, I choose thee for the mother of my soul, in honor of God's good pleasure in choosing thee for His Mother. Queen of men and of angels, I accept and acknowledge thee for my sovereign in honor of the dependence on thee as His Mother in which the Son of God, my Saviour and my God, willed to live. And in that capacity I give thee all the power over my soul and my life that according to God I can give. O holy Virgin, look on me as thy creature and through thy goodness treat me as the subject of thy guidance and the object of thy mercies.

"O Source of life and grace, refuge of sinners, I have recourse to thee to be delivered from sin, to be preserved from eternal death. May I be under thy guardianship, may I have a share in thy privileges and may I obtain by thy glories and privileges and by the right of belonging to thee, what because of my offences I do not deserve. May the last hour of my life, which will decide my eternity, be in thy hands, in honor of that happy moment of the Incarnation when God became Man and made thee Mother of God.

"O thou who art both Virgin and Mother! O sacred Temple of the Divinity! O marvel of heaven and of earth! O Mother of my God! I am thine by the general right and title of thy greatness, but I wish to be thine also by the special right of my choice and free will. I give myself to thee and to thy only-begotten Son, Jesus Christ Our Lord. I wish to pass no day without giving Him and thee some special homage and marks of my dependence and servitude, in which I desire to die and to live for ever" (prayer of Cardinal Pierre de Berulle).